Perplexed

CHRISTINA STARKEY

Just Chrissy

ISBN: 979-8-9995210-0-2

DEDICATION

For the one who taught me what it means to stay soft in a hard world.
For the moments that made me question everything
and the ones that made me believe again.
For the lessons learned in silence, confusion, and in-between spaces
too small to name.
Thank you for being a chapter I didn't see coming
and one I'll never forget.
This is for everyone who has ever felt trapped in their situation. You
are not alone. You can and you will get through this. I just want to
say thank you for walking through some of the most challenging
times of my life with me. You bring joy to my life and show me
every day how to be a better person. While my life was lived before
this book was thought of, you are the reason it's finally in action.
I hope you find healing in these words. You are enough. You are
worthy of breaking through the perplexity.

CONTENTS

Preface: Welcome to Complicated

Hey You,

If you're anything like me, you didn't pick up this book because life was going perfectly.

You're here because something feels messy. Complicated. Uncertain.

Maybe you're standing in a place where nothing makes sense.

Maybe you're tired of pretending you have it all figured out.

Maybe you're just exhausted from holding it together for everyone else.

If that's you... welcome.

This book is for you.

I don't have all the answers.

What I do have is a story... full of moments where life felt upside down and confusing... and the slow, sometimes painful, sometimes beautiful journey toward peace.

This isn't a step-by-step manual. Not a self-help book.

It's more like sitting on the couch with a friend, having the kind of conversation that feels like a deep breath.

Inside these pages, you won't find quick fixes or sugarcoated advice.

You'll find honesty.

You'll find permission to be human.

And hopefully, you'll find a little bit of hope.

So pull up a seat. Get comfy.

You don't have to have it all together to be here.

You don't even have to believe that peace is possible yet.

You just have to show up.

I'm so glad you did.

- **Christina**

Maybe you're facing stuff you never thought you'd have to. Or maybe

it's not one big thing... it's a million little things piling up.

Either way, complicated seasons have a way of making us feel stuck and totally overwhelmed. I get it... I've been there.

Here's the truth I had to learn the hard way:

Complicated doesn't mean impossible.

Complicated doesn't mean broken.

Complicated doesn't mean you're doing life wrong.

It just means...it's complicated. And that's okay.

Chapter 1 - It's Complicated

2 Corinthians 4:8-10

"We are troubled on every side, yet not distressed; we are perplexed, but not in despair; Persecuted, but not forsaken; cast down, but not destroyed; Always bearing about in the body the dying of the Lord Jesus, that the life also of Jesus might be made manifest in our body."

Hey Friend. Pull up a spot next to me. Grab your favorite snack, pull that throw blanket over your lap, and take a deep breath. You made it here. Right now, that's enough.

Life? It's complicated.

I know that you've been through it lately and probably have needed someone to just sit with you for a minute. I want you to imagine an oversized, comfy couch with tons of space to spread out on. We're both just hanging out with our favorite snacks/drinks and

3

about to dive into some things that might get a little heavy. **Just a small trigger warning:** Our time together might stir up some memories or emotions from your past. Some might have been long gone and seemingly dealt with, while others might be fresh and not worked through. Please do not mistake this book as a replacement for professional guidance. For now, I'd like to be your friend who hangs out and gives you something to think about.

I want to encourage you to keep a journal if you aren't already. Whenever you have questions, learn something about yourself, realize areas that need improvement, or experience positive moments that you want to celebrate, take the time to record them all. That journal will be your record of life. Of moving through the complicated times. The journal I keep has prayer requests and praises written in it. I date every entry at the top of the page, sort of like a diary. That way, I can go back through them and see all the crazy and amazing experiences I've had.

I speak from personal experience when I say that it's a huge blessing to revisit the words written during my most challenging times. Being completely honest and raw with myself, it was easy to want to give up and succumb to self-doubt. To believe that things were too hard to work through. Too hard to deal with. That there was no hope. That it was too complicated. What a word. Complicated. Seemingly impossible, and not very much room for hope. When we say things are complicated, it's easy to give up because trying to maneuver through whatever the issue is would require work. When I go back through my journal, I am reminded of all the times I have come out on top. Or how the super complicated situations seemed like they were never going to get figured out. With little time and intention, almost every situation I wrote about had an end that satisfied the need.

The title of this book is Perplexed. Merriam-Webster defines Perplex as - "To make unable to grasp something clearly or to think logically and decisively about something. To make intricate or involved: Complicate." How many times in your life have you felt perplexed by situations you were going through? Not only is it complicated, but it seems like you can't even think straight. Nothing about it makes sense. You don't even know what to do! I feel you, friend. Being in this headspace is hard. We so desperately want to come up with a solution, but we're just stuck wondering what to do! Can I offer a little bit of wisdom here? You're not alone. We have all experienced this feeling at some point or another. There are a bunch of moments in scripture where people were completely perplexed, too!

When I first set out to write this book, I had an ah-ha moment when I heard the scripture I will share with you. As I heard it for what felt like the first time, I was reminded of a song from back in my youth group days. It had all these cool dance moves that we kids would do together when the song came on. Who knew that 20 years later, a verse in this song would be the one that I would focus on to prayerfully help you through some of the most difficult times in your life?

Have you ever laid down, closed your eyes, and immediately fell asleep? In those moments, I am exhausted. Think of that word for a minute. Exhausting means to give your all completely. This could be your time, your gifts, your talents, or even every ounce of strength (mentally and/or emotionally) that you have left. It's possible that a job can be exhausting, sometimes even people. Then that tiredness can turn into frustration and even anxiety. Whenever you think about that person or situation, you start dreading your next interaction.

Something that we often overlook is that God wants us to cast all our cares on Him. Not just the big things like how you are going to eat or pay the bills. Those are all important, but the small things hold their weight equally. God wants to take the burden away from you because He loves you. The rest that He can give is so freeing. I like to think of it as a cool fall night by the campfire, drinking hot cocoa in a sweater, and the fire surrounds you with warmth, making you feel totally content. That is what God's love feels like to me every time I ask Him to step in and help me through overwhelming and complicated situations.

1Peter 5:7

"Casting all your anxieties on him, because he cares for you."

Matthew 11:28-29

"Come to me, all who labor and are heavy laden, and I will give you rest. Take my yoke upon you, and learn from me, for I am gentle and lowly in heart, and you will find rest for your souls."

Lord,

I'm so tired. I've been hurt, worked my tail off, and honestly..I just need a break. I ask that you give me rest. I just want to feel your love and take a break from being on edge all the time. Heal my mind and my heart. Thank you for taking my anxiety and stress away. Amen.

Reflection Journal: Chapter 1 - It's Complicated

When Life Doesn't Make Sense

You know what's funny?

When we hear the word "complicated," most of us think: Oh no, here comes the drama.

But what if complicated is actually the first sign that something in your life is about to grow?

Think about it:

- New relationships are complicated.

- Healing is complicated.

- Learning to believe in yourself again? Super complicated.

The best stuff in life usually shows up wrapped in a little bit of confusion and chaos.

A Couch Confession

I had a moment recently... sitting in my car, ugly crying in the

parking lot of a grocery store... where life felt like one giant tangled

ball of Christmas lights.

Nothing made sense.

Everything felt broken.

And all I wanted was clarity.

I sat there thinking, "God, could you just send me a flow chart?

An email? A clue?"

And in the silence, I realized:

Sometimes God lets us sit in the complicated on purpose.

Not to punish us. Not to confuse us.

But to teach us how to stay when we want to run.

How to trust when there are no clear answers.

How to breathe when all we want to do is hold our breath.

Why Complicated Isn't the End

The Bible is full of complicated moments:

- Noah built a giant boat before it ever rained.

- Abraham was asked to pack up his life and move without a destination.

- Esther walked into a throne room, knowing she might die, and she still said yes to saving her people.

None of them got a clean "this is what's next" memo.

They got complicated... and then they got called.

Maybe complicated isn't the end.

Maybe it's the beginning.

Before We Move On

I want you to hear me:

You're allowed to not have it all figured out right now.

You're allowed to sit in this moment with all its messiness and

unanswered questions.

But friend, don't give up just because it's complicated.

You're stronger than you think.

You're more loved than you feel.

And you're not stuck... you're becoming.

Prayer

Lord,

Sometimes life feels like too much. Too loud. Too heavy.

Help me to trust that even in the complicated, You are working.

Please give me the courage to stay when I want to quit.

Teach me to see Your hand even when it's not apparent.

Amen

Anchor Verse

"Trust in the Lord with all your heart and lean not on your own understanding."

-Proverbs 3:5

Reflection Questions

- What part of your life feels the most complicated right now?

- How have you been trying to handle it on your own?

- What would it look like to hand this complication over to God... even just for today?

- Write a prayer asking for clarity, patience, or peace in the middle of this complicated season.

Space to Reflect

Use the following blank pages to expand on these questions or anything that is weighing you down. Once you're finished, take 3 deep breaths. I know that this time of reflection will bring you clarity.

Chapter 2 - Tired of Hurting

At some point, we all experience our share of hardship or challenging times. It can be totally overwhelming when everything keeps going wrong. Somehow, you always manage to make it through. I know that sentiment all too well. When I was at my lowest, I remember being around a group of well-meaning people who told me things like "It will get better. Just give it some time. I would cringe a little when people said things like that.

One of the unique opportunities I have been given is that I have seen life from both sides of the coin. Not too many people often have that opportunity. Please hear me out, I am not trying to gloat or make myself sound superior. This is just my experience. I grew up in a home that provided me with everything that I could ever want, think, or imagine. We went on trips, took adventures, and enjoyed shopping sprees, living in a world of luxury with fast cars, boats, and more. No one ever knew how I lived my life. I had only a few friends, and those relationships were superficial.

Fast forward a few years, and the world as I knew it was completely ripped from underneath me. Everything in the blink of an eye was gone. On top of that, we were robbed and left with mounds of debt and no money. Nothing.

This wasn't just a rough patch, or poor rich person doesn't have their 5th car anymore. This was spaghetti 5 nights in a row. From steak house to $1 Salisbury steaks. Waiting in line at the local grocer to waiting in line at the church pantry for a handout. I remember digging through the car at one point just to find pennies to add as much gas to the car as possible. Just a drop to get us through the next few days.

I was angry, scared, sad, confused, worried, stressed, and lonely. Everyone who was once our "friend" stopped coming around. We didn't have anything to give.

I had recently started going to a local church because a new friend had invited me. Since we didn't have the money to be driving all the time, she offered to give me a ride on the nights that she was going to church. I remember apologizing to her all the time because it was actually out of her way to come get me.

One day, I was feeling really super down. We had gotten one of those pink slips in the mail. If you've ever gotten one, you absolutely know how I felt. For those unaware, it's like your stomach just drops. Everything you have worked for in your life is about to be ripped out from under you. The home and life you built are about to be taken away from you, leaving you with nothing. When we got to church, I was walking in the hall, and people were starting to greet me with smiles, and I couldn't hold it together anymore. I lost it right there in the middle of the hallway. My friend grabbed me and pulled me into the supply closet. She put both of her hands on me and told me to "spill!". I let her in on everything I could manage to get out through nasty tears and the snot explosion that was coming out of my face. She hugged me and told me that I'm not alone. She shared what was going on in her life, and I was amazed. "How are you still a person?!" I asked and declared all at the same time. She told me that it was people like me who helped her get through her day, and then said something that I will never forget: "You are a clean mouth in a room full of dirty mouths."

Every time we talked, I tried to encourage and lift her up. I wanted to find ways to show her that she could get through anything. Now it was her turn to show me that even though I was going through a tough time, there is always someone else going through their own personal hell. Wow. It changed my mindset forever. Was that time hard? Absolutely. It was so stressful and scary. Sometimes I woke up without power or had to shower at a friend's house. Even though it was tough, I'm glad I had that opportunity. I firmly believe that I am stronger than I ever thought I would be. That I can handle anything that life throws at me. That I am crafty. I am resourceful. I will get through this.

I started saying things like this to myself to affirm that I would get out of this, but at the same time, I accepted my current situation. I accepted the help that was available to me. My pride had to be broken. Asking for a handout was beneath me. I was the type of person who would help others, not the other way around. That very real wake-up call has shown me that we are all on the same level, just trying to figure it out.

So, I share all of that to show you that you are not alone. Please hear that. You might not be struggling financially right now, but it could be emotionally. I could tell many stories, but I'll spare you another day. But please believe that you are not alone. You don't have to go through this alone. Christ established the church so that they would care for one another. Some churches have the ability to help both the heart and the mind, and others have resources to assist financially or physically. I believe that accepting our situations and asking for help is the first step toward healing. If you aren't already, I encourage you to be involved in a local church. Find your "tribe" and hold each other accountable. Do life with them. Share your blessings and the hardships you are facing. Laugh, give thanks, rejoice, and mourn together. You can get through this. You are not alone.

James 5:14-16

"Is anyone among you sick? Let him call for the elders of the church, and let them pray over him, anointing him with oil in the name of the Lord. And the prayer of faith will save the one who is sick, and the Lord will raise him up. And if he has committed sins, he will be forgiven. Therefore, confess your sins to one another and pray for one another, that you may be healed. The prayer of a righteous person has great power as it is working."

1 Peter 2:24

"He himself bore our sins in his body on the tree, that we might die to sin and live to righteousness. By his wounds you have been healed."

Lord,

My heart has been heavy. I've experienced pain, loss, frustration, sadness, grief, and more. I give you all of my worries. I do this because I know that you can handle them and that you want to keep me in your care. Please show me how I can get out of my situation. Help me be obedient and turn away from toxic people and things. I've messed up, and I know I need your help. Please forgive me, Father. I ask that you break my pride if I am still holding on to feeling like I can't accept help. Soothe my heart and dry my tears. I am ready to receive your peace and work through my issues. Thank you for healing me, for forgiving me, and for showing me the way. Amen

Reflection Journal:

Chapter 2 - Tired of Hurting

Hey You,

If you've made it to this chapter, I just want to say... I'm proud of you.

Because hurt can be heavy. It can be the kind of heavy that makes even simple things... like brushing your hair or answering a text... feel like lifting a mountain.

And sometimes, being tired of hurting doesn't mean you're weak. It just means you've been carrying more than your share for too long.

The Quiet Kind of Tired

Let's be real.

There's a kind of tired that sleep can't fix.

It's the tired that seeps into your bones... the kind that comes from

pretending you're okay when you're not.

I remember standing in a room full of smiling people, nodding along

like I was fine, while inside I felt hollow.

You know that feeling? The "I'm here but not really here" feeling?

Yeah. That's the quiet kind of tired.

But listen: **God sees that version of you, too.**

Not the dressed-up, smile-for-the-crowd version. The real you...

tired, hurting, still standing.

Why Hurt Doesn't Mean Hopeless

There's a story in the Bible about a woman who had been bleeding

for twelve years.

Twelve years of pain.

Twelve years of doctors.

Twelve years of feeling overlooked and exhausted.

But one day, she did the bravest thing: She reached out anyway.

She pushed through the crowd and touched the hem of Jesus' robe...

believing that even the slightest connection could heal her.

And it did.

Friend, you might be hurting. You might be exhausted.

But you still have a hand to reach out with.

Even the smallest flicker of hope is enough for God to work with.

Couch Talk: Let's Get Honest

Can I be totally honest with you?

There were days when my prayers didn't even have words.

Days when I just laid in bed and whispered, "God, please."

No long-winded speech. No perfect theology. Just two words.

And you know what? That was enough.

Because the point isn't praying the perfect prayer... It's reaching out,

even tired and messy, believing that God hears tired hearts, too.

Tiny Signs of Healing

If you're tired of hurting, let's stop for a second and breathe.

Because maybe... just maybe... healing has already started in small

ways you haven't even noticed:

- You cried instead of holding it all in.

- You asked for help (even if it scared you).

- You smiled, even if it was just for a second.

- You chose to keep going.

These are not small things. These are signs of life, of healing

happening beneath the surface.

Prayer

Lord,

I'm tired. I'm hurting. I'm not sure what healing even looks like right

now.

But I know You see me.

Help me to reach out to You, even when it feels hard.

Remind me that I don't have to have it all together to be loved by

You.

Amen.

Anchor Verse

"Come to me, all you who are weary and burdened, and I will give

you rest."

-Matthew 11:28

Reflection Questions

- Where in your life are you feeling the most worn out right now?

- What are you tired of pretending doesn't hurt?

- If you could imagine laying down your hurt for just a moment, what would you hand over first?

- What kind of rest do you think your soul is craving today?

Space to Reflect

Use the following blank pages to expand on these questions or anything that is weighing you down. Once you're finished, take 3 deep breaths. I know that this time of reflection will bring you clarity.

Chapter 3 - Jumbled Words

A few years ago, a friend and I attended a faith conference. I'm not entirely sure how I discovered it, but I ended up with two tickets and a desire to learn. Walking into the conference space was a little overwhelming. Apparently, this was an event that many people were excited to attend. The whole front section of the conference was packed, and I found it challenging to get two seats together. I could see a few spots left towards the back of the hall. Worship started, so we grabbed two seats under speakers hanging from the ceiling and entered into the time of prayer and praise.

As the last song of the set was finishing, the main speaker was introduced. Then the wildest thing ever happened. From that moment on, I had no idea what was being said for the rest of the evening! It was like God completely turned off my ability to understand words, or that this guy was speaking in an unknown language that everyone else around me was in on. I sat there confused and wondering how this could be edifying to the church if I couldn't even understand a single thing that he was saying. After about 15 minutes, I decided to get up and walk around. Maybe the speakers above us were blown? It didn't matter where I stood in that room, I simply could not make sense of anything the guy was saying. I thought..ok, this is it. I've lost it.

Going into the hallway, I looked for anyone to say hello to. I just needed to verify that my brain wasn't completely broken. As soon as I left the room, there was a group of chatty women, and I could hear everything they said. "Ok, I've not completely lost it." I thought to myself. After a few more minutes, I returned to my seat and resumed the conference. I can see people in the room clapping. As I walk through the doors, the speaker starts up again. I still could not understand him! Accepting my fate, I returned to my seat and asked my friend if she was having a good time. She smiled and nodded yes, trying to get me to stop talking so she could continue listening.

I realize that this experience is pretty intense, but I bet you can relate. Sometimes it feels like no matter how hard you listen or try to make sense of a situation, everything seems so jumbled.

Complicated. Perplexed even. Maybe it's not actual jumbled words that you are hearing, but you feel like it doesn't come out right, no matter what you say. Have you stopped to think that maybe you weren't meant to hear or say what is trying to be said? I want to call this a life hack, but it's pretty obvious to most people. To me, it was life changing. Did you know that you don't have to fix every single problem that comes across your path? That sometimes it's ok to leave things complicated. I'm sure you've heard this before, but things have a way of working themselves out sometimes.

Remember when I walked out of the conference room to take a break from the confusion? I could clear my head, make sure that I was okay, and take a minute for myself. Instantly, I could hear the people talking in the hallway. I no longer felt like I was listening to someone speaking an unknown language. I was able to clear my head and just be present in the moment.

Reflection Journal:

Chapter 3 - Jumbled Words

Hey Friend,

Ever been in a situation where no matter how hard you try to make

sense of it, it's just... jumbled?

Like you're standing in a room full of noise, but none of it translates?

You nod along, you smile, you try to get it... but deep down, you're

thinking, I have no idea what's going on here.

Yeah. Me too.

When Nothing Makes Sense

That conference I sat in on, honest to goodness, it felt like the

speaker was talking in another language.

No matter how hard I leaned in, tried to focus, tried to catch even a

piece of it... nothing.

I couldn't process a single word.

At first, I panicked:

What's wrong with me? Why can't I understand? Why does this feel

so foreign?

But when I stepped outside for some air, it hit me:

Maybe I wasn't supposed to understand right then.

Maybe the confusion was its own kind of message.

Mental Hallway Breaks

Sometimes, you must step out of the noise... not forever, just long

enough to clear your head.

I call them mental hallway breaks.

You pause.

You breathe.

You get out from under the noise and just be for a second.

Confusion isn't always a bad thing.

Sometimes it's just a sign that you're overloaded.

That your mind and your heart need a beat to catch up.

Even in the Bible, People Felt Lost

1 Corinthians 13 says:

"For now we see only a reflection, as in a mirror; then we shall see face to face."

Translation?

Right now, life is a little blurry. It's not crystal clear.

But someday, it will be.

That gives me so much comfort... knowing that confusion isn't the end of the story.

It's just a chapter.

Couch Talk: Trusting the Blur

If we're being honest, the most challenging part of confusion is not knowing.

Not knowing what's next.

Not knowing if you're doing the right thing.

Not knowing how it all fits together.

But here's what I'm learning:

You don't have to understand everything to trust God with it.

You don't have to figure it all out today.

You can trust even in the blur.

A Little Life Hack

If you're feeling like everything's jumbled right now, here's your permission to:

- Step outside.

- Turn off your phone for a while.

- Take a deep breath.

- Remind yourself: Confusion is temporary. God is constant.

Prayer

Lord,

Sometimes life feels so noisy, so confusing, that I don't even know where to start.

Help me to pause.

Help me to trust that even when things don't make sense to me, they make sense to You.

Give me peace in the middle of the mess.

Amen.

Anchor Verse

"Be still and know that I am God."

- Psalm 46:10

Reflection Questions

- What areas of your life feel jumbled or unclear right now?

- How comfortable (or uncomfortable) is it for you to sit still in the middle of the confusion?

- Write about a time when something that once confused you finally made sense. What changed?

- Is there a quiet place in your life where God might be whispering?

Space to Reflect

Use the following blank pages to expand on these questions or anything that is weighing you down. Once you're finished, take 3 deep breaths. I know that this time of reflection will bring you clarity.

Chapter 4 - Perplexed but Not in Despair

"We are troubled on every side, yet not distressed;

We are *perplexed*, but not in despair;

Persecuted, but not forsaken; cast down, but not destroyed; Always

bearing about in the body the dying of the Lord Jesus, that the life

also of Jesus might be made manifest in our body."

-2 Corinthians 4:8-10

The key takeaway from this scripture that I want us to focus on is that they were perplexed but not in despair. Even though it is hard, it's not a complete loss. So while things might be a little complicated right now, remember that you've got someone who is rooting for you, who loves you, and will guide you through the muddy waters. Sometimes God's love looks like a friend who is inviting you to sit on their couch to talk through the difficult times. Even though you might want to throw your hands up and say that it can't be done, be encouraged friend. You're not done in this fight.

Have you ever met someone who instantly becomes a part of your story? Maybe they came into your life and suddenly fit in like they've been there all along. Or perhaps it was just for a very short time, but their impact will last for the rest of your life. That's exactly how I feel about my friend Elaina. The first and only time I met her, she shared an incredible story of being perplexed for the last 5 years. She knew that she had entered into a season of waiting and growth. Suddenly, opportunities started to line up, and she found herself in the middle of the woods as the caretaker for a family cabin. Can you imagine packing up and selling your belongings to move across the country and start over from scratch? Like quitting your job, leaving your friends and family, and starting a new life in the middle of nowhere. That's craziness! Of course, she was afraid, but she knew that God was setting her course. She knew that while there, she was meant to seek God and wait for wisdom. The crazy thing is that she knew she was meant to only stay at this cabin, and when it was time to come out of that season, she would know.

Year by year goes by, and she keeps to herself, waiting on God for the message that it's time. Five years passed, and she still stayed in the cabin, remaining faithful. One night, she was on the phone with her friends, and without talking to each other, both confirmed that it was time for her to come home. The craziest part is that they didn't even know that their friend was waiting for the exact words they said. She said that the time was completely set aside, and she felt closer to God than ever before.

Sometimes, too much noise swirls around us. Every person you meet has their own issues they are dealing with. When you get involved with someone else, you take on their issues. This can make it hard for you to see the path for your own life. It shows you how important it is to take time for yourself. You might not need to sell everything you own and move out to the middle of nowhere, but can we appreciate how great it is to get away for a little while to reset our minds and how we think about situations?

About a month after meeting my friend, the world shut down. I moved four hours away from everything I knew into a small house in the mountains and started my life over. A couple of months in, I was sitting on the back deck looking out into the trees, and it hit me.

I was living out the story that I heard from Elaina. I thought I was being silly when I thought, "I wonder if I'll be locked in for five years at this place, too."

What a funny thing to think. It's been 5 years since that moment, and looking back, I can see what God has prepared me for. He brought Elaina to me so I could be prepared for all the craziness that was about to happen. Her story gave me hope and reminded me of the reason for this time. Trust me, there were days when I did not want this cup to be passed to me. Why me? Why did I have to be sent away? Why did it feel like I was being ostracized from everything I loved? Stripped away from everything I'd ever known.

Then I realized it was because I needed to look at everything plainly. I needed to figure out if it's what I believed. If everything that I had told myself was actually true. It turns out that much of everything I knew was wrong. Not wrong in that it was awful and ruining my life, but wrong in the way it hindered my personal growth. There were so many barriers I needed to break down that I wouldn't have been able to see while I was still in the middle of everything. Sometimes we must be perplexed a little to take us outside our comfort zone. When things become too comfortable, we stop looking for flaws. We don't poke around to see if something needs fixing. There's always room for improvement, but sometimes we don't see that need until something is absolutely broken.

My life is meant to be shared so that other people can see themselves in my situation and gain hope, learn from my experiences, and hopefully avoid making the same mistakes I've made. I want to be a beacon. A light. I want people to see what I've gone through and my struggles, and to have hope that they can come out on the other side too. A little over a year ago, my best friend and I talked, and she told me that she felt like this was the year I would do great things. I was going to finally break out of what I've been going through, and I was going to live again. She had no idea I had been praying for somebody to say that to me.

As soon as she said it, it was as if my life was unlocked. Healing happened. I began traveling again, meeting new friends, forming new relationships, falling in love with myself, discovering my people, and finding my person. The entire year was full of life. It was completely contradictory to the last five years.

What you don't know is that I spent an entire year on the couch. I was sick and I didn't realize it. I was dying. Then one day, I got scared enough to go to the hospital, and they told me that I was anemic and I possibly needed a blood transfusion. That I need to start this new regimen. That I have been dehydrated for a very long time. The list just kept going on and on, and I had to start getting my blood drawn every three months get on this new healthy diet. It was a lot y'all. But I did scary things. I got out of the house. I drove again. If you know me, that's a wild thing because I'm a storm chaser. Just try to keep me from those many hours on the road. Spending an entire year not storm-chasing, traveling, or going out on adventures is wild for me. What's even crazier? The people in my life closest to me didn't see I had a problem. Make sure you surround yourself with people who genuinely care about your well-being. Those who can see your faults and aren't afraid to say something. If you see something, you say something. That is one of my biggest mottos right now. It applies to video games, but I'm seeing how this applies to life, too.

Reflection Journal:

Chapter 4 - Perplexed but Not in Despair

Hey Friend,

Let's be real... there's a vast difference between being confused and being crushed.

Perplexed? Sure.

Stressed? Absolutely.

Completely hopeless? Not today.

That's what this chapter is about... holding onto hope even when life feels upside down.

Troubled, but Still Standing

2 Corinthians 4:8-9 has been a lifeline for me:

"We are troubled on every side, yet not distressed; we are *perplexed*, but not in despair; persecuted, but not forsaken; cast down, but not destroyed."

Every time I read it, it reminds me:

It's possible to feel surrounded by problems but not be swallowed up by them.

It's possible to be confused but not crushed.

Despair Feels Like the End... But It's Not

Despair whispers:

- This is never going to get better.

- You're too far gone.

- What's the point?

But despair is a liar.

And here's the truth I'm learning:

Confusion is a classroom.

Pain is a teacher.

Perplexity is just part of the process... not the end of the story.

Couch Talk: Not Destroyed

I want to be honest... there were seasons when I didn't think I would

make it.

I wanted to quit. I didn't want to show up for my life anymore.

The world felt so heavy, and my hope felt so small.

But somehow, even on the days I was convinced it was over

...it wasn't.

And you know what?

You're here too.

Still breathing.

Still fighting.

Still choosing to read a book about hope instead of giving up.

That's not an accident.

That's proof that you're stronger than you think.

What Keeps You Going

If you're perplexed today... confused, overwhelmed, unsure how this could ever work out... know this:

Being perplexed is part of being human.

But being in despair is not your destiny.

The enemy would love for you to think you're defeated.

But God says you're delivered.

Look at the Legends

Paul was perplexed when he sat in prison cells with no clear end in sight.

Esther was perplexed when she faced the king, who was risking her life to save her people.

Ruth was perplexed when she left everything familiar to enter an unknown future.

But not one of their stories ended in despair.

Neither will yours.

A Truth to Hold Onto

You can be confused and still be called.

You can be exhausted and still chosen.

You can be hurting and still healing.

Prayer

Lord,

Sometimes I feel lost in the middle of my story.

But You say I am not destroyed.

Help me remember that confusion is not the same as defeat.

Teach me to lean into You, even when nothing makes sense.

Hold my heart steady when I want to quit.

Amen.

Anchor Verse

"We are hard pressed on every side, but not crushed; perplexed, but not in despair."

- 2 Corinthians 4:8

Reflection Questions

- Can you name a time when you felt surrounded but not destroyed?

- How did you find hope in that moment?

- What's one thing you want to remember the next time you feel stuck or overwhelmed?

- What does it mean to you that despair isn't your destiny?

Space to Reflect

Use the following blank pages to expand on these questions or anything that is weighing you down. Once you're finished, take 3 deep breaths. I know that this time of reflection will bring you clarity.

Chapter 5 - Choking Up the Growth

I'm not much of a gardener. One of my neighbors kindly let me in on that secret. She was very particular about how the yard was cut and would often leave notes or knock on the door to let me know that the grass got cut too much on her side. I'm talking about a max of 3 inches over the invisible line between our properties. She was a widow, and her children didn't come to visit her often, so I tried to have extra compassion towards her.

After binge-watching all of the home improvement shows, I decided that I was going to get some plants. Someone called me and asked if I wanted her to pick up some Knock-out Rose bushes. I was so stoked. This would be the first official plant that I've ever tended to.

I remember spending all morning digging up the dirt, filling the bottom of the holes with Miracle-Gro, transferring the roses over, and feeling so proud of my accomplishment. A couple of weeks later, my neighbor sent me a text (I figured it would be easier to air her grievances if I just gave her my phone number, and if she genuinely needed my help, I would be there for her). She asked if I would like to come over for a bit. I was a little shocked because up until now, I figured she hated me. I told her I would be over in a minute and met her between the houses. She invited me through the gate to her backyard and showed me her beautiful flowers, plants, and trees. She took great pride in tending to her garden. Then she said, "I can tell you don't know what you are doing. It might be good if I told you how to take care of your roses."

Instead of being overly offended and embarrassed, I exhibited a little grace and listened. She told me how important it was to get good light, proper water care, and how to tend to the growing vines. I thought the vines were just part of the plant, so I let them grow up. What I found out was that the vine was sucking the water, hogging up the sunlight, and choking out my roses. They likely wouldn't make it if I didn't get over there and prune them.

I didn't realize that so much went into helping them grow. I also didn't know that my neighbor was an expert in growing, but it showed me how important it is to know where you are planting your seed. You have to be so very intentional. Sure, you could pick a random spot and hope it takes root. Most likely, it will die. You could overwater it. It's gonna die. Let the vines choke it out. Dead. Finding good soil, caring for the plant, and tending to it is the only way it has a chance.

That day, I learned that my neighbor and I started on rocky ground. Anything said would spring up and then wither. It took time and care, but our relationship blossomed, and so did my KO Roses!

"And he told them many things in parables, saying: "A sower went out to sow. And as he sowed, some seeds fell along the path, and the birds came and devoured them. Other seeds fell on rocky ground, where there was little soil, and immediately they sprang up since they had no depth of soil, but when the sun rose, they were scorched. And since they had no root, they withered away. Other seeds fell among thorns, and the thorns grew up and choked them. Other seeds fell on good soil and produced grain, some a hundredfold, some sixty, some thirty."

-Matthew 13:3-8

Reflection Journal:

Chapter 5 - Choking Up the Growth

Hey Friend,

Let's talk about growth for a minute.

Not the pretty, Instagram-worthy kind of growth.

I mean the real kind... the kind that's messy, uncomfortable, and painful.

Because here's the thing no one tells you:

Before you can grow, you've got to clear out the stuff that's been choking you.

The Hidden Vines

When I planted my first roses, I had no idea what I was doing.

I thought they'd grow if I just put them in the ground and watered them.

Simple, right?

Wrong.

Turns out, there were all these sneaky little vines wrapping around the base of my plants... stealing the sunlight, sucking up the water, and slowly strangling the life out of them.

They didn't look dangerous at first. They looked harmless. Pretty, even.

But left alone, they would've killed my roses.

Couch Talk: What's Choking You?

We all have vines in our lives, don't we?

Little things that seem harmless at first but end up draining us:

- That toxic friendship you keep excusing.

- The habit you thought was "no big deal."

- The thought patterns you never challenged.

They wrap around slowly. Quietly.

Until one day, you realize:

I'm not growing anymore. I'm surviving.

And friend, you were made for so much more than just survival.

Pruning Hurts... But It Heals

I didn't want to cut back those vines.

I worried: What if I mess it up? What if I cut too much? What if the roses don't survive the pruning?

But here's the wild thing about growth:

Sometimes it looks like letting go.

Sometimes it feels like cutting away.

And as painful as pruning can be, it's also where new life begins.

Jesus even talks about this in John 15:2:

"Every branch that does bear fruit he prunes, that it may bear more fruit."

What Needs Pruning?

Maybe for you, pruning looks like:

- Setting a boundary.

- Saying no when you're used to saying yes.

- Letting go of a relationship that isn't helping you grow.

- Releasing a dream that's no longer aligned with who you're becoming.

It's scary. It feels unnatural.

But pruning isn't punishment.

It's preparation.

A Little Reminder

If something is choking your joy, peace, and purpose...

it's okay to cut it back.

It's okay to make room for better things to grow.

Prayer

Lord,

Help me see the things holding me back... even if they seem small or

harmless.

Please give me the courage to prune what needs to go.

Help me trust that in the letting go, you're making space for

something better.

Amen.

Anchor Verse

"Every branch that does bear fruit he prunes, that it may bear more

fruit."

-John 15:2

Reflection Questions

- What's something that feels like it's choking your growth right now?

- How do you usually react when life asks you to prune... resist, ignore, or lean in?

- What would it look like to gently release what's not serving you?

- What new things could grow if you made room for them?

Space to Reflect

Use the following blank pages to expand on these questions or anything that is weighing you down. Once you're finished, take 3 deep breaths. I know that this time of reflection will bring you clarity.

Chapter 6 - Show Me a Sign

There have been so many times that I just wanted a sign to know that I was on the right path. Anyone with me on this? Have you ever asked for signs? Have you ever been desperate enough to ask because you wanted to know that you're doing the right thing? I started looking for signs in simple things like animals, birds, road closings.. stuff like that. I didn't want to seem like a crazy person, so I didn't think that every single thing that I came across was a sign. Hence, I had to make sure that I was super specific about what I was asking for, so that whenever it happened, I would know that this was a sign from God.

I would write it down in a notebook, sign it, and date it. That way, whenever it happens, I could look back and say, "Look, the prayer was answered!" At first, the signs were straightforward. It could be something like a bird or a color, or something that I would know, something that I asked for. When I was deciding to move from a rental home into my mortgaged home, I asked for a cat to cross my path. Here's a funny thing about God: sometimes He gives us signs, and the way that He wants to give them, so you have to keep your eyes open.

I knew that I had to call my realtor that night with my final decision before 9 PM. It was about dinner time. If I wanted to see a cat cross my path, I needed to go outside. So I loaded up the car and went for a drive. I drove for hours, then I realized that I probably wouldn't see a cat. I became frustrated and upset because I felt this was the next step, but I wanted God's confirmation that I was supposed to do it. So I turned around and headed back to the rental. It's almost 9 o'clock, time's up. As I turn towards my street, I see some cars backed up. It's a truck with a super long trailer that is backing into one of the houses off the main road. He's completely stopped traffic. The car in front of me turns, and that puts me right behind the truck and trailer. As I'm about to roll my eyes, be frustrated, and say some not-so-kind words, I realize that this truck is carrying a skid steer. You know the Caterpillar brand? Yeah, this is in big yellow and black letters: CAT. Oh my goodness!! I got back to the rental as quickly as I could and called the realtor. I submitted my offer, and within half an hour it was accepted.

That was the beginning of the crazy signs. I want to tell you, though, that before this experience, I hadn't had big signs like this. It took me being intentional, asking, and seeking to realize that this was possible. I feel like sometimes we want to ask for a sign, or we want to ask for assistance or help, because everything around us seems so chaotic, but then we don't do anything to find the sign or seek the help. Had I just stayed inside the house? I wouldn't have seen a cat or the caterpillar machine going across the road. Had I stayed inside, I wouldn't have had the confirmation that this was the home I was supposed to purchase. I would have been sad, gone home, and completely missed out on that opportunity. Then, over the next five years, my life would have been drastically different. That one simple prayer, the act of not giving up, and the determination with expectancy is what helped me through one of the most confusing times of my life.

When I say I was perplexed, I really mean that. This was during the time that the world was shutting down. It seemed like everything around me was just dead ends, confusion, and fear.

Everything was telling me that this shouldn't work out, because nothing was going right during that time. Who buys a house in the middle of a pandemic?! Fast forward a month later, I'm sitting in the parking lot of the title company, and someone walks out a clipboard for me to sign papers. I essentially bought my home from the inside of my car.

Something I am learning is that the biggest blessings, most exciting adventures, and craziest experiences don't come naturally or normally. Most of the time, I have no idea what I'm doing. I might be confused, but I know that when I trust in God, He will light my path and guide me. Why? Because I've seen him do it so many times before. It just takes that little bitty bit of faith for him to show us amazing things. I think you can do that. I think you can muster up the strength to say to God, "I have no idea what I am doing, but I know you do. Please help me. Send me a sign. Show me what I'm supposed to do, how I'm supposed to do it, where I'm supposed to go. The people who are supposed to be there, Lord help me."

Every time things start to get hard, we need to reach out to God. Tell him exactly what is on your mind. "God, things are so rough right now. This is terrible. My life sucks. I hate it. I hate it here". Those are the prayers we might be used to praying. I want to challenge you to dig a little deeper. Start by asking God these questions:

How can I get out of this situation?

Show me how to do this.

Bring me the right people.

Give me the signs so that I know.

We need to combine action with our faith. We can't just believe God's gonna bring me through it. God's gonna do it. Yes, He will, but we have to put our action in it too. I had to go out and seek, not just sit in my room and pray. I had to believe that he was going to bring it to me even when I gave up. It seemed like all was lost. I dropped my shoulders and went back home, and then he came through. Now I know from my example it seems like, "well, you gave up". I'll be honest, yes I did. I didn't think that I had gotten the sign. The time was really close, so I decided to head back. That's a lesson in itself. God doesn't work on our timeline. He works on his time and in his perfect timing. He knew what time I needed to get back to call the realtor. He knew that He was going to put that cat in front of me. How funny is it that this was the first random thing that came to mind when I was like, "OK, I'm gonna ask for confirmation. Show me a.........cat!" It wasn't something big and magical and crazy out there. It was just the first thing that I could think of. Make your prayers simple. Quit trying to overcomplicate things, quit trying to perplex yourself even further! There is no confusion within God.

Since I've been getting these signs, I've been trying to ask for even more specific things. Lately, I've been getting signs without even asking. The craziest one that I think I've ever experienced was not too long ago at the car wash, of all places. This is something that I would go ahead and tell anybody, let alone write in a book, but I feel like God gave me this experience so I could share it with you. Plus, I have confirmation from someone who was with me, so I don't feel quite so crazy.

It had just recently snowed, so I took the Jeep out on some trails to learn how to maneuver on ice for the first time. Needless to say, it needed a wash badly. I decided to take it to the car wash for one of those fancy spot-free rinses. As we pulled into the car wash, I realized I had pulled too far to the left, which meant the soap would be heavier on one side. It was too late to back up. The machine was already starting, so I just put it in park and let it do its thing. It's one of those super fancy multicolored strobe lights, kind of car washes. Never really quite understood why a car wash needs a rave inside of it, but I'm not here to complain. It begins with a pre-rinse, followed by a mixture of soap and water. Then it starts spraying tricolor foam all over the jeep, making it look like a rainbow of foam.

I'm living my best life, taking in the beautiful colors and hearing all the sounds. As I looked over to my passenger side, I noticed that the soap was only two-tone on the windows. Purple and blue. Thinking that this is weird because the rest of the car was just yellow. I kept my eye on it. Is this a sign? Then, a couple of seconds later, the soap starts to melt downwards. First, it's the purple on top, and as it melts away, I notice something. It's spelling out my middle name. I kid you not. I gasped so loud and pointed and said, "What do you see?! What does that say?!" My passenger looks at the window and confirms that it is, in fact, my middle name. Freaked me out. This was like the writing on the wall kind of thing. What does it mean? Why do I see my name? Was it to get my attention, because it definitely worked! We are both bewildered in this moment. Then a couple of seconds later, the blue starts melting down, and it works out the word sapphire. So I point again and say, "Look!". We both saw it. Thank goodness I wasn't by myself because I would've thought maybe the fumes from the car wash were getting to me. This was just one of the coolest experiences I've ever had, but what does it mean?

Sometimes, signs can be confusing. So even if you ask for a sign or if one is given to you, it may not make sense right away. Continue to seek. Continue to ask for its meaning. Don't just hear it and then think, "OK, that was a cool sign", and then move on. Sometimes God will use a sign multiple times over and over for years.

As if the signs from the car wash weren't enough to get my attention, I began to see signs everywhere. One time, I prayed specifically for a Texas Roadhouse to be built in the parking lot where I was standing, and not even six months later, the land was gated off with a huge sign saying "Coming Soon! Texas Roadhouse." Now ask me what I asked confirmation for. I didn't write it down! I thought, this is such a big sign that if it ever happened, I would know for a fact the answer that God was giving me. I was in awe, so I started asking for more signs. One day, I was trying to think of something that would be so random, so out there that if I saw it happen, I would know that it was God (again). I was driving home and said, "If it's a yes, then build a roundabout right here." There's literally no reason for a roundabout to be there. There aren't any others on that road. I'm pretty sure the closest roundabout is a half hour away. Kid you not. One random night while driving, I noticed a road construction sign that said to expect delays due to an upcoming traffic circle. You have got to be kidding me. A ROUNDABOUT?! Guess what, I didn't write that one down either. I learned my lesson after that one, though. Every time I ask for confirmation, I write it down in my notebook.

Reflection Journal:

Chapter 6 - Show Me a Sign

Hey You,

Let's be honest... have you ever begged for a sign?

I know I have.

Not just once, either. Plenty of times.

It usually sounds something like:

"God, if I'm supposed to do this can you, like, send a sign?

Maybe a giant blinking arrow? Or a skywriter?

Or literally anything?!"

Yeah. Same.

Signs in the Small Things

Sometimes we think signs have to be huge and dramatic... like thunderbolts or burning bushes.

But a lot of times, they show up in the simplest ways:

- A song you needed to hear.

- A random conversation with a stranger.

- A closed door you didn't expect.

One of the most unexpected signs I ever got was from a skid steer... you know, a construction machine?

I asked God for a "cat" to cross my path if I was supposed to make a big move in my life...

and what rolled right in front of me? A CAT-branded machine.

Not exactly what I had pictured... but exactly what I needed.

Couch Talk: What Are You Looking For?

Here's the thing:

It's not about the sign being perfect.

It's about the faith it takes to ask for one and the trust it takes to notice it when it comes in a way you didn't expect.

Sometimes, we're so focused on how we think God should answer that we miss the way He actually does.

Signs in the Bible

Gideon asked for a sign... not once, but twice.

Moses saw the burning bush.

The shepherds followed a star.

God's not against giving signs.

But sometimes the sign comes after we move... not before.

It's faith and action working together.

When the Sign Isn't What You Expected

Can I be real for a second?

Sometimes you get a sign... and it's not the one you were hoping for.

- The relationship ends.

- The job falls through.

- The move doesn't happen.

But even then... especially then... God is speaking.

Closed doors are signs, too.

They're mercy in disguise.

How to Look for Signs Without Losing Your Mind

Here's what's helped me:

- Ask God boldly but humbly.

- Be specific, but stay open.

- Look for peace... not just perfect circumstances.

- Trust that "no" and "not yet" are signs, too.

One Last Thing

You don't have to chase signs to prove God is speaking.

He's already with you.

Sometimes the most significant sign is the peace you feel in the middle of the chaos.

Prayer

Lord,

I'm looking for You... not just for signs, but for Your presence.

Help me trust that You are speaking, even when it's quiet.

Open my eyes to see what You're showing me, even if it's not what I pictured. I trust you fully.

And please give me peace, no matter what the answer is.

Amen.

Anchor Verse

"Whether you turn to the right or to the left, your ears will hear a voice behind you, saying, 'This is the way; walk in it.'"

- Isaiah 30:21

Reflection Questions

- Have you ever asked God for a sign? What happened?

- How does it feel to trust God even when the sign isn't clear?

- What would it look like to believe that He's guiding you, even when it's quiet?

- Write about a time God answered in a way you didn't expect.

Space to Reflect

Use the following blank pages to expand on these questions or anything that is weighing you down. Once you're finished, take 3 deep breaths. I know that this time of reflection will bring you clarity.

Chapter 7 - 5 Mountains

I have a really cool story that I want to share with you. It happened a long time ago, but it affects me every single day of my life. I was in college, and I would come home on the weekends to hang out with my friends and the young adults ministry. We had a small group that would meet up in people's homes. It was really cool. It felt like we were doing something different.

One weekend, we were invited to the leader's house because there was a man who was going to come over and teach us about prophecy. Now, I had never been prophesied over or really had anything to do with prophecy up until this point. I had seen it on TV and had my own feelings about whether it was real or not. So when this man went around the room and started offering words of wisdom to all of my friends, I was a little standoffish.

I just want to break the fourth wall here for a second and let you know that all of the prophetic words that this man said came true.

Although I'm still working on mine.

He's going around the room. Every single person was having an emotional response. I felt really awkward about it, so I didn't want to get prophesied over. I sort of tucked myself back into the hallway. This man was sitting on the couch in the other room, he really couldn't see me. He had gone through everyone, and they were now singing worship songs and just hanging out. Then this man goes, " I've missed someone. Who have I not prophesied over? God has a word for someone still. Who did I miss? God has a word for someone still. Who did I miss?"

Oh, I tucked myself even deeper into that hallway. My best friend Niki points me out and says, "Here! Over here! She hasn't gotten prophesied over yet!" I rolled my eyes so hard. I thought to myself, I'm okay, thank you. I don't need it. He said, "Oh no! God's got a really big plan for you." He asked me to come into the middle of the room so everyone could see because this wasn't a normal prophetic word. Of course! Why would it be? Why would anything that has to do with me be normal? Every single other person that he had prophesied over had a straightforward word for them. He put his hands on one person and was like, "You're gonna use your hands to heal people." Get this. They were in the medical field, and he didn't even know that these two people were together. He said, " You're gonna work together, doing the healing, and doing the notetaking." Fast forward a few years, and they got married and worked in medicine together. To my best friend, he told her that she was going to be a mother to many children, and she absolutely did. To her boyfriend at the time, he told him that he was going to bring healing to people through his musical talents. He is in a band now. Playing in the places that most people wouldn't go. He might not realize it, but he's providing life to people. All the people in that room had very specific words of wisdom given to them. I'm sure you're interested in hearing what this man had to say about me. Of course, I will share with you, but strap in for a wild journey.

He begins to explain that he sees me standing on top of a mountain, like on the tippy top of the mountain so very high up, and he stops and pauses to explain that it looks like I'm Mickey Mouse. You know from Fantasia. He says he sees me there, staying on top of this very tall mountain, raising my arms up, and every mountain that's around me, all different colors, are rising up. He said it was as if I were controlling each of these five mountains with power, wisdom, strength, and money. He began to explain that my reach would go far beyond what I could ever see. That I was a leader, that I was going to make a humongous difference. He said he just kept seeing me controlling all these different areas, and that God would provide every single step of the way. He said that some people might be jealous because of how easy it may seem. That I'll have so many different opportunities. But he wanted me to know that God would guide me.

And that was it. Can you just be here with me in this moment when I say that was downright perplexing? What in the world am I supposed to do with that? Everyone else got a clear answer. You're gonna be a mom, you're gonna be a musician, you're gonna be in the medical field. Points to me and says you're Mickey Mouse!! I get it. I get the mountains now. Fifteen years later, as I'm sitting literally on a mountain writing this book, I get it. I prayed for confirmation on this prophetic word, and someone with no connection to this individual, who had never heard what he said about me, recorded a 10-minute audio for me about what they were hearing from God.

Not only did they mention the five fold ministries, which line up with the five mountains that the other man was talking about, but they also went into more detail about things that they saw from God that were going to happen in my life. Books, television, businesses, faith-based, ministries... so far, everything is lining up.

I share this with you because even though I had an idea of what life was going to look like, it was still very much the most confusing thing I've ever heard. Why couldn't it be easy? Why couldn't He just tell me, "You're going to write books, you're gonna be on television"? Why couldn't He just tell me all these experiences that I was going to have, so that I could confirm them later? God doesn't work the same for every single person. He knew exactly what I needed to hear in that moment so that I would continue to seek him out. God knew that it couldn't be easy for me. I have been seeking the meaning of the mountains for 15 years. That in itself is a blessing. My faith has been expanded. It wasn't easy. Every step of the way was confusing and complicated, and often, I didn't know if I was on the right path or not. But God always finds a way to gently guide me back onto the path and help me see that He is guiding me. There have been times when I thought I had reached my limit. He's done with me. It's over.

But it's never like that.

Just like the scripture says, we're perplexed, but not in despair. Of course, it's frustrating. Of course, I don't have an idea of what I'm supposed to do. But I'm never really lost. The difference here is that we are the ones giving up. God isn't giving up on you. He stands at the door and He knocks. He's waiting for you to come to him. He wants to know how your day is. Your week. Your month. The last decade. He's waiting to hear from you. Don't let the mountains of unknown scare you away from the path that He has for you. Just because it sounds silly or doesn't seem as straightforward as others directions, stay the path.

I've been thinking about this book for a while, and how I wanted to share some of these stories with you. I don't even want to come across as having all this incredible wisdom, that I am some Sage who knows everything. I often tell people I know a little about a lot, and a lot about a little. Faith happens to be one of those things that I know a lot about. Mainly because I've been through some pretty crazy things, and Faith was the only thing that got me through it. You might have some scary mountains in your life right now that you are perplexed by, and you have no idea how you're going to get through this. I want to encourage you not to give up. It may seem hopeless. It may look like there's no way out.

Recently, I had a pretty big setback while I was on a trip. My Jeep started overheating, so I took it to a shop. After a long day of being tossed around by different mechanics, we found that it was the head gasket. Oof. If you're familiar with cars or repair costs, this one stung a bit. While I was standing in the garage getting the bad news, the mechanic turned to me and said, "You know about Mount Everest, right?". I nodded, I had seen it in books and on tv, but never in person. He began to share with me that it is 29,000 ft. That many people spend their whole lives trying to climb it. The wild part? The last 40 feet is when most people give up. Not because they are tired, but because they can't see the path in front of them. The most challenging part of the climb is called the Hillary Step. This was a 40ft vertical rock that would turn many away. Can you imagine getting all the way up there and just turning away because it seems impossible? Just a short climb and they would summit. They would reach what they have worked for their entire lives. The mechanic turned to me and said that God has me here for a reason. Sometimes we have to go through the storms in life to appreciate what is on the other side.

Friend. You can do this. You will get through this. The confirmation will come. You will find your way. Take a moment if you haven't already done so, open up that journal that we talked about at the beginning of this book, and write down what your biggest mountains are in your life right now. What are the things that scare you? What is it that you feel is holding you back? What's the big goal that you have that you can see out in the distance, but you have no idea how you're going to get to it? Spend some time today writing out all of your fears, all of your worries, and all of your confusion. At the end of your entry, write a prayer to God asking him to guide you and bring you peace.

Reflection Journal:

Chapter 7 - 5 Mountains

Hey Friend,

Let's talk about mountains.

Not the hiking kind (although, huge respect if that's your thing).

I'm talking about the life kind... the ones that stand in front of you,

daring you to climb.

The ones that look too big, too steep, too impossible.

If you're facing some mountains right now... you're in good

company.

The Vision of Five Mountains

A long time ago, someone gave me a prophetic word... a vision of me

standing on top of a mountain, arms raised high, controlling five

different mountains around me.

It sounded wild at the time.

I didn't understand it.

Honestly? I laughed it off.

But looking back now, I get it.

Each of those mountains represented an area of life I would have to grow through.

And none of them were small.

Couch Talk: Your Mountains Matter

Maybe your mountains look like:

- **Faith Mountain**... Trusting God when the road is unclear.

- **Healing Mountain**... Letting go of old wounds.

- **Courage Mountain**... Facing fears that have held you back for years.

- **Purpose Mountain**... Stepping into a calling that feels too big for you.

- **Rest Mountain**... Learning to stop striving and just be.

Whatever your mountains are, here's what you need to know:

They are climbable.

They're not there to crush you... They're there to grow you.

Mountains Aren't Punishment... They're Preparation

It's tempting to see obstacles as punishment, as if you're being tested or picked on.

But what if mountains are invitations?

Invitations to become stronger.

To see how high you can actually go.

Without the mountain, you wouldn't know the view from the top.

Without the climb, you wouldn't know the strength already inside you.

Biblical Climbers

Moses had Mount Sinai.

Jesus had the Mount of Olives.

Even the greatest leaders had to climb before they could lead.

The mountain isn't the end... It's the proving ground.

What Your Mountain is Teaching You

Maybe it's teaching you patience.

Or humility.

Or boldness.

Or trust.

Whatever it is, it's not wasted.

Not one hard step.

A Little Challenge

If you're staring up at your mountain right now, here's what I want you to remember:

- Don't measure your progress by how fast you climb.

- Measure it by the fact that you're still climbing.

One step at a time.

One faithful choice at a time.

One brave prayer at a time.

Prayer

Lord,

These mountains feel big. Sometimes bigger than me.

But I know You're bigger.

Please give me the strength to keep climbing, even when the top feels far away.

Remind me that You're with me on every step of the climb.

Amen.

Anchor Verse

"Truly I tell you, if you have faith as small as a mustard seed, you can say to this mountain, 'Move from here to there,' and it will move."

- Matthew 17:20

Reflection Questions

- What feels like your biggest mountain right now?

- What fears come up when you think about climbing it?

- What's one small, faithful step you could take this week toward that mountain?

- How might God be using this mountain to grow you?

Space to Reflect

Use the following blank pages to expand on these questions or anything that is weighing you down. Once you're finished, take 3 deep breaths. I know that this time of reflection will bring you clarity.

Chapter 8 - 67-Foot-Tall Jesus

A change of scenery is usually something that really helps me when I'm going through stressful times. Currently, I'm going through one of the most challenging seasons of my life, so I'm finding myself traveling a lot more than usual. During one of my recent journeys, I discovered a place in northern Arkansas that features a 67-foot statue of Jesus. During the year, they have plays of the passion of Jesus, and they have a mock Bethlehem that you can go through with actors and scenes. It's actually a pretty cool place, but during the winter everything is shut down except for the museum and the statue.

Driving up to the statue feels like a spiritual journey. I parked farther away than most people probably do because I wanted to hike to Jesus. I wanted to take that time so that I could be thinking in my head about all the craziness that's been going on, because I want to entirely focus on him and hopefully find some sort of wisdom. As I'm getting closer, all of these birds just start squaking. I'm talking hundreds of birds. What you might not know is that God sends birds to people as signs. Different birds have unique meanings, so I was trying to figure out specifically which birds were making noises, but there were so many that I couldn't really hone in on more than just a few. I could hear that some of them are warning calls. Some of them were mating calls. It seemed like a mixture of distress, but also of peace. That is pretty much how I was feeling at that exact moment. As I got closer to the statue and turned to where my face is now looking at Jesus's face, the squawking stopped. It is completely silent.

Out loud, I said, "OK, I'm here. What do you want me to know? What is it that you want me to see?" I stand there patiently, dead center of this giant statue, staring at it, and not even 10 seconds later, I hear this noise behind me of shuffling feet. It sounded a little erratic, so I turned my body to look, and it was a kid. The weather that day was pretty chilly, so I was bundled up in a jacket, socks, and shoes. This kid was wearing shorts, a T-shirt, and no shoes or socks. I'm thinking, what's wrong with this kid? Then I realize that there's no one else around me, so where are his people? He starts running around the area, babbling things out loud. I can't really understand him, but as he gets closer, it's like the understanding came.

Now I'm gonna say this, I don't think that I have the gift of the interpretation of tongues, but in that moment it was like I understood what he was saying. I knew that he was babbling and speaking in an unknown language of some kind, whether it was just made up or if it was actually something else, but the more he said, the more I could understand him. He ran in front of me, and then way up by the statue, then back behind me, and then all over again. I'm just smiling because I know that this is God. Right, I know that he put me here in this moment because there is something that I am supposed to see or hear.

The kid comes right up to me and pokes me in the arm. Then he points to Jesus and points back at me. He says, "God is big! God loves you!" I smiled and agreed. Yes, He loves us! Then it was almost as if he was saying no no no you're not listening.. "He is big... He loves us!!" Then he shows me the tip of his thumb while squinting to emphasize how little his thumb is and points to Jesus, how big He is. And I understood that he was telling me Jesus is so much bigger than all our problems. All the things that I'm going through that my thumb is just this little tiny piece of me that is so insignificant. My issues are so small compared to the love that he has for us. The kid then says Mother Hawk, while pointing to Jesus. I'm not too sure what all that means just yet. I did do some light Google searching, and it seems like it could mean protection, which I mean, we all know that Jesus is all about that. Perhaps he was trying to say that Jesus is watching over us like a hawk and has a motherly love to take care of us.

I might be reaching, but it was a cool thing to hear him say that. A few moments later, this red SUV pulls up and hollers out, "Elijah!!". Of course, this kid's name is Elijah. The mom gets out of the SUV, walks down the hill, and gets her kid to come with her back to the SUV. As they're walking, the kid is babbling all the same words he said before, and the mom understands every single thing that he says. She's saying "yes I know God is big, he loves us, yes, Jesus's mother Hawk. A picture? You want me to take a picture of you and Jesus. OK here we go. Good job. OK, let's go. We can come back another day." Just like that they leave. No more sound, no more no more birds shuffling feet, no more babbling. Just complete silence.

In this moment, you can say that I was pretty perplexed. There was nothing logical about what just happened. I tried to make sense of it all, but it ended up confusing me even more. I knew that God wanted me to see all of that, but I couldn't figure out why. It's not like I learned anything drastically amazing that I didn't already know before. Nothing was really a confirmation for me. It was just a unique experience. But at the same time, it felt like there was something huge there, so yeah, I was pretty perplexed. I feel like the times in my life when my spirituality is super high, that's when logical things take a backseat. If I sit in my rational brain too much, then I end up attempting to think my way out of a faith-based situation. Meaning, I'm going to try to prove God wrong. What a concept. Proving the existence of God. Maybe not his existence, but his intention on how he plans to connect with me. I feel like we need to turn off the logical brain sometimes and connect with the Faith brain. Sometimes it doesn't make sense. Sometimes it absolutely seems impossible, and there's no way to prove it. That's why we have to have Faith. Believe the inconceivable. Faith without seeing.

Reflection Journal: Chapter 8 - 67-Foot-Tall Jesus

Hey Friend,

Let's go on a little trip together... to a place where the quiet is thick, the air is crisp, and standing tall in the middle of it all is a 67-foot statue of Jesus.

Yeah. You read that right.

A Journey I Didn't Know I Needed

I was in one of those heavy seasons... you know, the ones where you don't even realize how much you're carrying until you finally set it down.

I packed up my car, turned the music low, and just drove.
No real plan.
Just me, the road, and a heart that needed to breathe.

That's how I ended up in northern Arkansas, standing at the base of a giant Jesus statue, feeling small and seen at the exact same time.

Couch Talk: Sometimes You Have to Change Your View

Sometimes the best thing you can do for your soul is change your scenery.

Not run away... but step away.

Get quiet. Get still. Get somewhere you can see things a little differently.

Standing there in front of that statue, I didn't hear a booming voice from heaven.

I didn't get a skywriting miracle.

What I got was a deep, gut-level reminder:

God is bigger than this.

Bigger than my heartbreak.

Bigger than my fears.

Bigger than my messy, complicated life.

Signs and Silence

As I stood there, birds scattered and squawked overhead... all noisy chaos.

But the closer I got, the quieter it became.

Until there I was... face-to-face with Jesus... and everything went still.

In that moment, it was like God whispered:

"You're here. I'm here. That's enough."

Sometimes we're waiting for fireworks and flashing lights.

But more often than not, God shows up in the stillness.

Biblical Quiet Moments

Elijah didn't find God in the wind, or the earthquake, or the fire.

He found Him in the whisper.

And sometimes, so do we.

A Kid Named Elijah

I'll never forget what happened next.

A little boy... no shoes, no socks, just pure joy... came running around

the statue, babbling in a language I couldn't understand.

But somehow, I knew what he was saying.

He pointed at Jesus and at me and said:

"God is big. God loves you."

And just like that, it clicked.

I didn't need a sign.

I didn't need a solution.

I just needed the reminder:

God is bigger. And He loves me.

What the 67-Foot Jesus Taught Me

You don't have to have it all figured out to be fully loved.

You don't have to clean up your mess to be seen.

You don't have to climb your way up to God... He's already standing with you.

Prayer

Lord,

Thank You for being bigger than my problems.

Thank You for loving me even when I'm a mess.

Help me to remember that You are always near... even in the silence.

Teach me to trust in how Big your love is for us and rest in Your presence.

Amen.

Anchor Verse

"Be still before the Lord and wait patiently for him."

- Psalm 37:7

Reflection Questions

- When was the last time you felt tiny... in a way that made you trust God more?

- What distractions keep you from noticing His presence?

- How might your life feel different if you slowed down enough to really notice Him today?

- Write a prayer thanking God for being bigger than anything you're facing.

Space to Reflect

Use the following blank pages to expand on these questions or anything that is weighing you down. Once you're finished, take 3 deep breaths. I know that this time of reflection will bring you clarity.

Chapter 9 - Chase the Storm

There's been this town that I passed through about 10 years ago, and every time I hear that name, I know that God is blessing that situation or whatever I'm going through at that exact moment. If I hear that name, I know whatever is about to happen is going to be good. If I'm supposed to go there, I know that it's about to be a blessing. I might see roads, buildings, or parks. It could be anything with that name, and I know that God is about to do something for me there.

I really love chasing storms. Probably one of my favorite things to do during the summer is to check the radar and notice a pop-up storm that is close enough to chase. The last storm I chased, I kept feeling like something was off. For some reason, I just wasn't feeling like I should be out there. I would try to get in front of the storm, and then my car would slide around, immediately reminding me that I should just go home. I started to listen to that voice, and I pulled over into a concrete car wash. The wind was blowing at about 65 mph, and I watched tree limbs tumble across the parking lot and a transformer exploded like fireworks. Thinking that the worst was past me, I decided to get back on the highway and try to get in front of it again. I have radar in my car so I can see how close I am to the leading edge of the storm. I heard the prompting again. "Just go home. Call it off. You've seen enough."

I decided to ignore those feelings and continued on down the highway. The rain started pouring, and I mean pouring. It was like I was on my very own personal tidal wave ride, and its newest feature was to dump buckets of water so fast that you can't see anything. Just then, a semi cut over in front of me. I was trying not to get frustrated with the truck driver. So instead, I tried to show a little bit of thankfulness and said, "See, God always sends me a semi." This was about the fact that, often, when road conditions have been terrible due to fog, flooding, or freak hail (all of which have happened), there would randomly be a semi that would come almost out of nowhere, and I could get behind it to be guided through the hazard.

A couple of seconds later, this semi decided that he didn't

want to stay in this lane because the car in front of him was going too slow, so he changed lanes. I was cruising behind him in his tire tracks, so I decided to switch lanes with him. As soon as I got over the cars that were behind me got up to speed with me and were now getting stuck like we were. I noticed that ahead of me looked really foggy all of a sudden, and the wind started blowing like crazy. The cars next to me suddenly stopped. It caught my eye, so I looked over and saw a full-grown 70-foot tree completely blown over into the right lane of the highway. I'm not even kidding you. That would have been me. Either that tree would have gotten me, or I would have run into it if it wasn't for that semi. I would have gotten around the slow dude and found myself in a dangerous situation. I called off the chase and immediately alerted the police and reported the damage on the roadway.

I tell that story for a couple of reasons. 1. Never ignore the gut feeling. That still, small voice was the Holy Spirit. God was trying to get my attention to send me home, but I kept ignoring it. 2. God saved me that day because He is good. Not because of anything that I did, but because it was His will.

2 Timothy 1:7

"For God gave us a spirit not of fear but of power and love and self-control."

Romans 3:23

"For all have sinned and fall short of the glory of God.."

Ephesians 2:8

"For by grace you have been saved through faith. And this is not your own doing; it is the gift of God.."

Reflection Journal:

Chapter 9 - Chase the Storm

Hey Friend,

Let's talk about storms.

Not just the ones outside... though I do love chasing a good summer

thunderstorm... but the ones that hit inside us, too.

The ones we don't always see coming.

The ones that rattle our bones a little.

The ones that leave us wondering if we should've just stayed home.

The Thrill and the Risk

If you've never chased a storm before, let me tell you... It's a wild

feeling.

You're flying down back roads, radar pulled up, adrenaline high.

You're trying to get close enough to see the power without getting

swept away by it.

And honestly? Life feels a lot like that sometimes.

We chase dreams.

We chase healing.

We chase love.

We chase the life we think we're supposed to have.

But sometimes, in the middle of the chase, we realize:

Maybe this isn't the storm I'm supposed to be chasing.

Couch Talk: Knowing When to Pull Over

There was a storm I chased once where everything inside me
screamed turn back.

I ignored it.

I pushed on.

And right when I thought I was outrunning it... a tree came crashing
down right where I would've been if I hadn't finally listened and
pulled over.

That moment stuck with me.

Because sometimes the bravest thing you can do isn't chasing the storm... It's admitting that it's time to pull over.

Listening to the Whisper

God doesn't always shout.

Sometimes He whispers:

"Turn around."

"Wait."

"Not this one."

But if we're too caught up in chasing, we miss it.

And friend, missing it can cost you more than you realize.

What Are You Chasing?

It's worth asking:

- Are you chasing validation from people who'll never give it?

- Are you chasing a dream that doesn't fit anymore?

- Are you chasing approval, success, love, healing... but ignoring the whisper telling you to rest?

Not every storm is meant to be chased.

Some are meant to be weathered... safely, quietly, with God leading the way.

God Sends the Semi

In my storm chase story, God didn't send an angel with a trumpet to stop me.

He sent a semi-truck to slow me down.

Literally.

Sometimes, grace shows up looking less like a miracle and more like an annoying traffic jam that saves your life.

A Different Kind of Courage

Real courage isn't always chasing after what's loud and flashy.

Sometimes it's listening to the quiet nudge saying:

Wait. Trust. Let Me guide you.

Prayer

Lord,

Thank You for being the whisper in the middle of my chase.

Help me to know when to run, when to walk, and when to be still.

Teach me that not every storm is mine to chase... and that sometimes,

You're saving me by slowing me down.

Amen.

Anchor Verse

"The Lord will fight for you; you need only to be still."

- Exodus 14:14

Reflection Questions

- Think about something you've been chasing hard lately. Have you stopped to ask if this is still where you're supposed to be heading?

- What would it look like to pull over, even just for a moment, and check in with God?

- How do you know when it's time to press on... and when it's time to pull over?

- What would it look like to trust that God's timing is better than yours?

Space to Reflect

Use the following blank pages to expand on these questions or anything that is weighing you down. Once you're finished, take 3 deep breaths. I know that this time of reflection will bring you clarity.

Chapter 10 - Beauty of Perplexity

As a youth pastor, I knew that each summer during youth camp, it was well known that on Wednesday night of the week, there would be this overwhelming 'come-to-Jesus' moment. I used to think that it was fabricated in every church camp across the United States that had worked together to make Wednesday night Holy Spirit night. It became sort of a runnin inside joke that we knew that Wednesday night was going to be the holiest of holies. There would be an altar call urging everyone to come to the front either to give their life to Jesus for the first time or to be filled with the gifting of the Holy Spirit. Everyone would be in tears, and it would be a beautiful yet predictable event.

One particular summer, I was going through one of the most difficult times of my life, and I didn't have the patience or the time to deal with another Holy Spirit night. I say this because I wasn't sure how authentic this experience was. I had attended several of these Holy Spirit nights, but for some reason, I never received what everyone else was receiving. I wouldn't have the spiritual breakthrough that everyone else had. No speaking in tongues, interpreting, miraculous healings, or any of the other gifts were happening in my life. I'll admit, it was cool to see lives being changed around me, but I wanted something real. I wanted my life to be changed. I wanted my situation to be better. I didn't want to go somewhere that was predetermined that everyone's gonna fall in love with God this night. Everything's going to get better and then we're going to leave this bubble, the safe place that we've created, and go back into the real world where life is going to suck. I didn't want it.

On that particular night, I decided to sit back. I let all my friends go down to the pulpit, do their thing, cry out to Jesus, pray the prayers, pray in tongues, sing the songs, have this incredible worship experience. I sat back. I sat there and wondered why God wasn't moving in my life. Why he felt so distant to me. Why it felt like everyone else around me was having this fantastic experience, and I was just existing. Sometimes I feel like we get caught up in our thoughts and create a self-fulfilling prophecy that we won't succeed. We are going ahead of ourselves to make sure that we fail. Can you just let that sink in for a moment? We desperately want to succeed in every area of our lives, and we ask God to guide us, but yet we're secretly trying to make sure that we fail behind the scenes. Why do we do this to ourselves? Is it because we don't want to see ourselves succeed? Are we punishing ourselves for sins or for our shortcomings? Or is it because we believe that we are so terrible that we don't deserve goodness?

I think that's where my problem is with myself. I have been surrounded by so many toxic, religious leaders, pastors, churches, ministries, you name it. I had been taught to believe that I was so inherently evil that no good could come from me outside of God. That only through Jesus would I be able to accomplish something great. Now I'm sure that might sell in Books and that might sound good from a pulpit, but I don't think that that's true. I believe that God creates beautiful things. I think that you are beautiful and not a mistake, and I don't feel that your shortcomings make you a terrible person. I think we are just people who make awful decisions sometimes. The longer I sat back from my friends and everyone who had gone down to pray, I felt this strong magnet drawing me to do something great. I felt like God was speaking to me, but I didn't want to hear him because I was so wrapped up in my own situation that I was mad at him. I was creating this atmosphere that I didn't want to hear from God.

That's not even true. I love God. I love seeing him work in my life and in the lives of people around me. It's the coolest thing to see people get healed from years of trauma or even from a sickness that they've been dealing with. That same week, my best friend Niki had lost her voice. This man approached us as we were walking to the chapel and began talking to us. She whispered to him that she couldn't speak as she was pointing to her throat. After a few days of team competitions and worship time, she had completely lost her voice. The guy thought that was the coolest thing ever because if you're going to lose your voice, it should be singing praises as loud as you can to God.

This guy then tells me to put my hand on my friend, and we were going to pray and believe that she would be healed and that her voice would come back. Within a minute, he's telling her to start speaking and to start praising God, and I heard her voice go from nothing to something. It sounded like a high-pitched whisper, very breathy, to a full-bodied voice. She was able to continue singing, talking, and sharing her testimony for the rest of the summer, both during church camp and on the mission trip.

I know you've seen God do amazing things through other people in your own life, so I know that you can relate to this. Sometimes it's easier to see where God is working outside of ourselves. For whatever reason, when it comes to us, it's hard to see where God is moving in our own lives. As I sat in the pew, watching everyone down at the pulpit, I knew that God was calling me to full-time ministry. I didn't want it. How would God use me? This ultimately, messed up person, who has a track record of sinning, lying, manipulating, controlling, not trusting, and running away from God at every chance I could get. On the outside, it looks like I was a perfect kid, but inside, I didn't want to be here. I was struggling. I felt like nobody could relate to me. That I was just too messed up, too tarnished, too damaged, that God couldn't use me.

Why would he want to use damaged goods?

If I could just talk to my younger self right now, I would beg her to hang on a little bit longer. I would tell her that she is exactly where she needs to be and that God wants to use her exactly as she is. That she's beautiful. That the temptations and the frustrations and the shortcomings she's dealing with right now are only temporary. That one day she's going to get understanding for all the things she's gone through, and it will give her power to overcome all of the issues she's dealing with. That she lied to protect herself. That lying wasn't her and didn't make her a terrible person.

I know that sounds a little weird to you because you don't know my whole story, but to protect myself, I will just say that I had to lie because I was told to. I was made to become this person so that I wouldn't get hurt. I had to carry that with me every single day of my life because I so desperately wanted to tell the truth, but every time that I got a little bit of courage to say something, I would be reminded that I would ultimately get hurt if I did. I know somebody can relate to that. I know how deeply that hurts. I just want to give this moment a piece of wisdom:

You don't have to stay stuck.

You can tell your truth.

You can find your people.

You will be safe.

You can leave.

If that makes sense to you right now, awesome. I know that you're going to get it. To everyone else, take it like this: The situations that you get put into in life are meant to teach you something. Sometimes that lesson might not be for you specifically. It might be for someone you'll meet years down the road. The next time you encounter a stressful situation, don't just view it as an inconvenience. It might be confusing. It might seem like there's no hope, it might feel like you're up against Giants. In the future, when you're looking back on it, you'll realize that you had strength the whole time.

That's the beauty of perplexity. Things don't make sense. Nothing seems logical. You might even feel like everything that is happening to you is existing outside of time. Yeah. I know that hits deep. Take a moment to write in your journal some of the things that have perplexed you to the point that it didn't even seem real. What is something in your life that is still bothering you? Maybe you don't think about it every single day, but what's the thing that happens every so often? When you're just going on with your life, it hits you, and you get stuck for a little bit. Take a moment to write that out and then ask the question: Why? What was its purpose? Do you see it yet? Ask yourself why you think it happened and seek out the meaning that is there for you. I promise that the more intentional you are about sitting down and reviewing some of these life moments, the more you'll start to see patterns and recognize areas where you might not have failed if you had caught on to the situation sooner.

Gotta give a shout out to my best friends who I play video games with every single day of my life. I never knew that I would learn so much more about myself as a person, as a member of society, as a friend, than I would by playing video games. We get on every single night, and we play as Spartans saving the world from an invasion. I know that sounds so goofy, but I love these guys. We are a team. We get on our headsets, call out what we see, and help each other improve. Now, these guys have been playing together for over 10 years, so I'm coming in a little late to the game. They still treat me with respect and have shown me how to become a better team player. It's about focusing on your movement. Be intentional about where you want to be positioned. Knowing the spawn areas means knowing where our opponents will appear in the game and remembering effective game strategies so that we can work together to win. All of these things are super specific to this game, but when you think about it, all of this applies to life in a huge way.

Focusing on your movement and positioning in life is vital to figuring out who you want to be and where you want to go. If you want to expand and grow and be something in this life, you can't just sit in your bedroom. You've got to reach out and find people, you got to put yourself in places that lead you closer to where you want to go. If I have this big dream of being a mountain bike rider, I'm going to have to buy the bike. I'm going to have to go on a trail. I'm going to have to journey across the United States to the most beautiful places that have the most scenic vistas, so I can truly feel part of the mountain bike community. Staying at home watching YouTube videos does not accomplish this. Take the challenge and get outside of yourself. Stop being so afraid to fail. It may look confusing and like you're surrounded on all sides, but you won't ever know unless you push through.

Knowing the spawn areas and memorizing the game strategies apply to every situation in life too. When you know that there are people in your life who cause roadblocks or pull you down, you're going to want to avoid their spawn areas, the places that they hang out. Game strategies are created based on previous play. When you reflect on your life and consider the situations you've been in, you can develop strategies and boundaries to protect yourself.

Reflection Journal:

Chapter 10 - Beauty of Perplexity

Hey Friend,

Perplexed.

It's not exactly a word you put on a t-shirt or a coffee mug, right?

It's the kind of word that feels heavy... a little tangled, a little frustrating.

It's not a place we want to live.

But what if... stay with me here... what if there's a kind of beauty hiding inside perplexity?

What Perplexity Feels Like

Perplexity is that space where life doesn't make sense:

- The doors that slam shut.

- The relationships that fall apart.

- The plans that crumble.

It's confusing. Disorienting. Exhausting.

But it's also... sacred.

Because it's where we learn to trust.

Couch Talk: Blessing in the Complicated

I used to think the goal was to get through the hard seasons as quickly as possible.

But looking back, some of the best, deepest parts of my story were built in seasons when I didn't know what was going on.

It was the confusion that made me ask better questions.

It was the waiting that stretched my faith.

It was the uncertainty that taught me how to listen.

Perplexity isn't the enemy.

It's the classroom where hope, patience, and grit are born.

Biblical Beauty in the Mess

Think about Joseph.

Sold into slavery by his brothers. Forgotten in prison.

Perplexed? For sure.

But later, he looked back and said:

"You meant evil against me, but God meant it for good."

-Genesis 50:20

The beauty didn't show up in the easy moments.

It was woven through the confusion... the questions...

The long, winding road.

The Beauty We Almost Miss

If we only ever lived in the clear, easy parts of life, we'd miss:

- The strength that grows in uncertainty.

- The friendships forged in fire.

- The faith that survives the dark.

The beauty of perplexity is that it strips away the noise and teaches us what really matters.

Let the Perplexity Do Its Work

If you're confused right now... if life feels like a thousand tangled knots... take a breath.

You're not broken.

You're being built.

You don't have to figure it all out today.

You don't even have to like it.

You just have to stay open to the idea that beauty could be hiding here, too.

Prayer

Lord,

Thank You for working in the messy, confusing parts of my life.

Help me to trust that even when I don't understand, You're still writing a good story.

Show me the beauty hiding in the places I least expect.

Amen.

Anchor Verse

"He has made everything beautiful in its time."

... Ecclesiastes 3:11

Reflection Questions

- What's something confusing in your life that might actually be shaping you?

- How have you seen beauty come from confusion in your past?

- What would it feel like to believe that even this messy, perplexing season is part of a bigger plan?

- Write about one area of your life where you're asking God to show you the beauty.

Space to Reflect

Use the following blank pages to expand on these questions or anything that is weighing you down. Once you're finished, take 3 deep breaths. I know that this time of reflection will bring you clarity.

Chapter 11 - Thief of Joy

Has anyone ever REALLY gotten under your skin? I mean, they just did something so ridiculous that you just about lost it? Oh, trust me, I have been there. I could share so many stories, but I'll keep it short. One day, I was out storm chasing, and I was coming up to an intersection at a fairly busy route. I was waiting for my turn to cross three lanes of traffic and two turn lanes. All of a sudden, this backwoods blessed son-of-a creation comes up quick behind me. I see the break in the traffic, and I am accelerating to take my turn. This dude straight up almost ran me off the road. I'm not even kidding you. I had to swerve into the ditch, barely missing the stop sign. My windows were open. I yelled out...ARE YOU FLIPPING KIDDING ME?!?!?! Dude proceeded to tell me I was number 1.

Every part of me wanted to find him, take down his plates, and go full Karen mode. He needed to learn, and I was about to teach him. It took me a minute to cool down, and then I was able to rationalize. No, I did not tear across the highway looking for him. I realized I was reacting to a situation I had no control over. My following him to give him a piece of my mind or "turn him in" was not going to take away the fact that it happened or fix him. I pulled over and prayed for him. Why? Obviously, this guy was in a hurry. Was it cool? No. You know what was even more not cool? The fact that I let someone shift my attitude so quickly caused me to react in a way that I wouldn't want to.

I want to share this quote with you that has kind of changed my life.

"Comparison is the thief of joy."
-Theodore "Teddy" Roosevelt

Wow. Let that sink in. *Read it again.* Do you get it, really? The THIEF. What do we know about the thief? "The thief comes only to steal and kill and destroy; I have come that they may have life, and have it to the full." - John 10:10
Where do you find your joy?

For a while, I told myself that I would never compare myself to other creators. However, I quickly noticed that when I wasn't "trending," I would hop on their social media accounts to see how I could change who I was to gain more attention. Yes, I just admitted that out loud. I would spend <u>hours</u> looking at their profiles, trying to mimic what they were doing. Why? So I could become Insta-famous? For what?

I realize that not everyone cares about their social media presence, but this applies to everything in life. Whenever you put yourself up against someone else and think of yourself as less than, you are (unfairly) comparing yourself. The reason we are who we are is due to our experiences. That person that you are comparing yourself to most likely has had their share of hardship or sacrifices just to get to the point that they are at now.

The most important thing we can do is learn to find value in ourselves, in our story, and in our journey. We must remember that God is the one who blesses us and takes us through life. He's the one who gets the credit because this life isn't possible without Him. In that same vein, we must also find our purpose in Him. When we start looking around and comparing ourselves to other people, we are actually taking the focus off of God and idolizing others. Back in the OT days (Old Testament), when the followers would fall away, they were usually losing their focus on God and creating idols for themselves that they would pray to. They literally thought that a piece of wood was going to fill their requests of being a "Good enough _____".

Take time today to write down all the things that God has gifted you with. What is special or unique about you? How are you different than others? God made you special for a purpose, on purpose. Next time that you start to compare yourself to others, I hope you remember that God made you unique because He has a special journey for you that you wouldn't be able to complete if you were anyone else. You were made wonderfully in His sight. He picked you out. He hand chose you. You were knitted together with precision. Everything about you was created in a way that honors God and brings about a greater plan to help others. Why would you ever want to be anyone else?! Of course, we can always strive to better ourselves, but always remind yourself that you are who you are, and that is good enough.

Lord,

Sometimes I don't feel like I am good enough. I've let others down, and sometimes I feel like I have even let you down. When I look at other people, it sometimes seems like they have it all together and possess everything I don't. I'm not perfect. Father, I ask that you show me how I am special in your eyes. Help me to love myself the way that you love me. Show me how to use my unique talents and gifts to help others. If there's anyone that I want to strive to become, it's you.

Help me to love deeper and breathe slower. Thank you for reminding me that I was created for a reason and that you love me just as I am. It's hard to hear that sometimes because this world is full of people who expect others to earn their love. You have given your love freely. I am so thankful that you love me for who I am, and that you see me and still love me.

Amen

Reflection Journal:

Chapter 11 - Thief of Joy

Hey Friend,

Joy can be a fragile thing sometimes, can't it?

One minute you're feeling good... you've got peace, you're smiling, you're maybe even laughing a little.

And then... bam... something sneaks in and steals it right out from under you.

Joy thieves are real.

And the sneakiest part?

Half the time, we don't even realize what's happening until the joy is already gone.

Spotting the Joy Thieves

Some of the biggest joy thieves in my life haven't been loud or obvious.

They've been quiet little things:

- Comparison.

- Bitterness.

- Overthinking.

- Fear.

- Perfectionism.

It's wild how fast a good moment can crumble when you start looking around instead of looking up.

Couch Talk: The Comparison Trap

Let's be real... comparison is one of the fastest ways to wreck your joy.

Scrolling through someone else's highlight reel when you're sitting in your behind-the-scenes mess? Brutal.

But here's what I'm learning:

Comparison will always make you feel like you're losing... because you're playing a game you were never meant to play.

God didn't make you to be a copy.

He made you to be a creation...

original, messy, beautiful, fully loved.

Guarding Your Joy

In John 10:10, Jesus says:

"The thief comes only to steal and kill and destroy; I came that they may have life, and have it abundantly."

Joy is part of that abundant life.

And it's worth protecting.

You don't have to hand over your peace every time life throws you a curveball.

You can stand guard over your heart.

You can name your joy thieves and start locking the door.

Setting Up Boundaries

Sometimes protecting your joy looks like:

- Saying no when you're used to saying yes.

- Unfollowing people that trigger comparison.

- Stepping away from conversations that leave you drained.

- Choosing rest when you feel pressured to hustle.

You're allowed to guard your joy.

You're allowed to protect your peace.

Joy is a Rebellion

Choosing joy... in a world that thrives on negativity and

comparison... is an act of rebellion.

It's a declaration:

I will not let the hard things steal my hope.

I will not let the noise drown out my peace.

I will not give away my joy without a fight.

Prayer

Lord,

Thank You for the gift of joy... even in hard seasons.

Help me recognize the things that steal it away.

Teach me to guard my heart and protect the peace You've given me.

Let my joy be a light that points back to You.

Amen.

Anchor Verse

"The joy of the Lord is your strength."

- Nehemiah 8:10

Reflection Questions

- What steals your joy faster than anything else?

- How can you set a boundary around your heart this week, month, year?

- Where do you feel God inviting you to protect your peace right now?

- Write about a joy-filled moment you want to hold onto tightly.

Space to Reflect

Use the following blank pages to expand on these questions or anything that is weighing you down. Once you're finished, take 3 deep breaths. I know that this time of reflection will bring you clarity.

Chapter 12 - From Perplexity to Peace

When it rains, it pours, right? Have you ever had days, weeks, months, or years like this? The plumbing breaks, the power goes out, the tire goes flat, and the car battery dies. All in the same day. In those moments, I have been known to just turn off all of the lights and go back to bed. The problem is that going to bed doesn't fix anything, so my crummy day turns into a crummy week or longer. Why do I give up? I think it's mostly because, in the moment, I feel like I "can't" do something. The idea that something or someone is too overwhelming (that I cannot do it) is incredibly frustrating. The ones that seem to hit the hardest are when I have a goal in mind and I fail, or I feel like it will never happen. In those moments when I feel like giving up, I know that I need to turn to God. So why don't I?

I really had to dig deep on this one, so hang with me. I believe we all share a sense of pride when we accomplish something. As children, we would run to the adults and show them our creations or something that we were extremely proud of, having done it all on our own. They would make their eyes all big and nod in an approving manner, and we would tote off, full of joy and a happy spirit. That's really the only reason why we shared our creations. We crave that positivity and attention. I feel that this is deeply rooted within us; when we don't achieve the sense of accomplishment we desire, it can lead us into a dark place.

James 1:2-4 says we will "meet trials of various kinds". I kind of like to replace that with, "deal with a bunch of crap that sucks.". We must have this level of expectation that when (not if) we get through this, we will emerge stronger. When the testing time is over, you'll be able to take that huge sigh of relief and be thankful that it's over. Then you'll be able to see all that you've learned along the way. The takeaway: Cast all your cares on God because he cares for you. (1 Peter 5:7) You were not meant to do this alone. Don't give up. You can do this.

James 1:2-4

"Count it all joy, my brothers, when you meet trials of various kinds, for you know that the testing of your faith produces steadfastness. And let steadfastness have its full effect, that you may be perfect and complete, lacking in nothing."

Joshua 1:9

"Have I not commanded you? Be strong and courageous. Do not be frightened, and do not be dismayed, for the Lord your God is with you wherever you go."

Lord,

I know you're there, and all I need to do is ask for your help. I'm losing my mind. I don't know how to handle the situation I'm going through, and honestly, I thought I could handle it on my own. Please help me figure out what I'm supposed to do. Thank you for always hearing me when I talk to you and going with me so that I am not alone. I need your true shalom (peace). Help me make it through this trial. Thank you for loving me.
Amen.

A majority of this book was written in the mountains of Arkansas. I set out in the morning to explore some trails, not knowing where I was headed. I have an app on my phone that showed me some trails north of where I was staying. It showed that the intensity was low, so I felt comfortable enough to go on my own. Typically, you don't go on trails by yourself because if anything were to happen, you wouldn't have anyone to help you out. I was wanting to stick to easy trails that were more like back roads, gravel dirt paths, kind of thing. The first trail that I went on was pretty basic. There was a low water crossing, so I got to splash some water over the hood. Then it led up to this big hill, which then took me into 11 miles of pure mountain. There's no power out there. There's no street lights. It's just you, a dirt path, and the mountain.

It seemingly goes on forever, even though it's only 11 miles, but you're in 4 low, only going about 10 miles an hour. At one point, I pulled off into the woods because I felt like it was time to write. I've had all these experiences in my mind for years. I knew that I wanted to write about them, but I never really knew the right time to bring it all together. This book has taken over five years to bring us together. When I first decided to write this book, I had no idea that I would end up with a Jeep and in the mountains, writing this book. But it makes sense for the moment I am in. My whole life, everything has been paved for me. Everything was just so. There were rules, and people were guiding me every step of the way. Everything was shiny, pretty, and new. Offroading is the complete opposite of that. You have a general idea of where you're headed. Everything is dirty. No power. No lights. No one to guide you. Everything is old. Organic. When you're out on the trail, no one can judge you. It's just you, God, and nature.

I heard the wind today. I heard the birds. I breathe in the crisp mountain air. I felt the sun on my skin. It had been so long since I connected with myself outside of society. While I'm writing this book, I'm having experiences that will be used for the next one.

For the next lesson.

Last year, when I got the Jeep, I didn't know how integral this hobby would be for my healing. It got me back on the road, which I haven't been doing since 2020. Before Covid, I was always out on the road. You might have seen me attending a concert, conference, or taking trips with my friends. For me to stay holed up in my house for four years sounds nothing like me. Once I got my wheels, I felt like I got my freedom back.

I started by going on trails because I like being in nature. Every time I sit in nature, I feel like I can actually think. So I'll find myself constantly trying to retreat and get away just so I can sit out in nature. One of my friends asked me where I was going this weekend, and I told them that I had found this cabin in the mountains overlooking a beautiful lake. He made fun of me because I always bring my Xbox to play video games with them. He says, "You drive 4 hours every weekend just to sit in a different house to play video games? Let's go!" Truthfully, I'll bring my gaming console to distract me from the thing that I'm supposed to be doing.

You know, like writing this book. When things get complicated or I have a moment of overwhelm, I retreat to something that brings me comfort, which is spending time with my friends or playing a mindless video game. It definitely makes it easier to play with them because they've been doing this for the last 20 years. Many of them are on leader boards. Some of them play in competitions pretty often. Now they've got me signing up for competitions!! Since they're really good at this game, it means that I don't have to put in that much effort when we play late into the night.

We'll get into this in a little bit, but think about the things that distract you so that you don't have to deal with the hard thing. What is it in your life that you have placed there, so that you can retreat away from reality instead of plowing through?

My life has been quite complicated lately, so I've been taking more drives and exploring Jeep trails. A couple of months ago, I went on my first water crossing. If you have no idea what that is, it is precisely what it sounds like. You're just taking your off road vehicle and crossing over a body of water. Most times, it's a small creek or stream, and the water doesn't even go over the tires.

The first big crossing that I did, the water was maybe a foot and a half deep. I remember being so scared that the water was going to sweep me away and that I would end up in some bog somewhere, unable to be pulled out. I pulled in, backed out, pulled back in, backed out again. Put it in park, walked around, decided that I wasn't educated or experienced enough to do this crossing, and almost backed down. In that moment, I realized that I had driven 2 1/2 hours to get to this place. I stayed up all night the night before planning out my coordinates so I could find it. I researched everything I could on water crossings, including how to put your Jeep in four-low and take your time, and I watched videos of people who had completed similar crossings. I was not going to leave the space until I crossed the stream.

Not because I had somewhere to go,

but I almost felt like I had something to prove.

Let's just sit with that for a second. Things may look complicated, and it may look like you have something to prove, but it doesn't mean that action is the best step forward. Sometimes, we might need to stop, get out, and walk around. Actually, get in the water and see how deep it's going to get. Not just plowing through the stream. Not just unquestioningly hoping that it's all going to work out, but by taking your shoes off and wading through the water just a little bit to see if you can handle it.

I crossed that stream so easily. I took my time, and the Jeep seemingly pulled me through to the other side. It was actually kind of magical. Then, when I was done, I stopped my video recording, put it in park, and replayed the moment. My heart was racing, and my hands were shaking just a little bit. Now I felt like I could take on any trail, any wild adventure.

I think that happens when we go through complicated times too. Once you've gone through the worst thing, small problems don't even look like they can affect you. But that's when we let our guard down. We think, oh, we've been through worse, so this is nothing. When complicated things or people appear in the future, you may not be guarded as much to get out of the Jeep. Take your shoes off and wade into the water. You might pause and look at it. Sort of size up how deep you think it really is, but then you just go all in. This is why boundaries are crucial when it comes to complex individuals and situations. It's not that you don't love that person or the thing that you were doing. It's a way to protect you.

On my latest off-roading adventure, I went through another water crossing. This one wasn't planned, and it wasn't part of a jeep trail. It's just due to the flooding that's happened in the area from all the recent rain. The local meteorologist said that we could expect 7 to 9 inches of rain to fall over the next couple of days. That caused a lot of flash flooding, and the water has settled down into these valleys.

As I was driving to my cabin for the weekend, I passed several roads that were closed and was even diverted from the road that I was supposed to take. I used my map to navigate around the neighborhood, avoiding the closed road, and I found myself in yet another area that had flooded. *Sometimes when you're trying to avoid people who cause issues in your life, you'll attract different people with similar issues.* The cycle continues. The difference is that when we have boundaries, we can control the narrative.

So, while I avoided my first road closure when I arrived at the second road that should have been closed, but there was no sign, I should have backed up and turned around. Instead, I thought, " I've done water crossings that aren't even this deep. This is nothing." I put the jeep into four low, slowly crept into the water, and rolled right along the path. The water was crystal clear. I could see the river rock and the concrete pad underneath. I learned that just because you can see the bottom doesn't mean that it's shallow. Just because you think you know a person doesn't mean you know the whole story. As I reached the halfway point of the stream, I realized that the water I thought was only 2 1/2 feet deep had actually increased to 4 1/2 feet deep. The water was going over the hood.

I just watched a video the night before of a Jeep stalling out in floodwaters. One of my friends was able to winch them up and pull them out. When he was explaining what had happened to those people and why they didn't make it, I paid attention. Sometimes it's essential to listen to the stories of people around you who have gone through hard times. You might pick up some wisdom to help you and your future endeavors. What I mean is that you might avoid some problems that you wouldn't have had to go through. Sort of a get out of jail free card.

When I was in the middle of the deepest water, I gasped. In a split second, I had two options. Either stop and put it in reverse, or plow forward and hope for the best. Looking back, it would have been wiser to take the opposite approach and find an alternative route. However, I learned a great deal about myself by plowing forward. My mind brought that comment to my memory. All I heard was 'keep moving forward if you don't want to stall out.' The coolest part about this adventure is that I recorded the whole thing. You can physically see the moment that my brain triggered, and I gave it some gas. The water started spilling over the hood, and I could feel it coming up from the floorboards. I knew that if I didn't give it gas, I was gonna get stuck here. If I didn't get out, it was going to be a problem.

Friends, sometimes when we're in the midst of a complicated situation, we have to make a decision. It's either all or nothing. Either you keep pushing forward, holding your head high and your shoulders back, or you need to stop and remove yourself from the situation. I find value in both scenarios. One might require a little more maintenance afterwards. Just like I'm going to have to make sure that my air filter is dry, that my fluids don't have water mixed in with them. I need to check my spark plugs to make sure there's no water being held in there.

There's a small list of things I need to do to ensure that my vehicle is okay. The same applies to us. After we go through a stressful situation, we owe it to ourselves to take care of it and do a little maintenance. That's gonna look a little different for everyone. Maybe you would like to go out in the countryside. Maybe shopping is your thing. Maybe sitting on your butt watching Netflix for eight hours straight with the curtains shut is what's going to bring you peace. Whatever that looks like, it's so important. You can't skip the maintenance if you're going to plow through complicated scenarios. If you don't, it could cause issues further down the road.

Tonight, as I sit in my cabin overlooking the beautiful valley and see the floodwaters below, I'm reminded of a very exciting adventure I've been on. I had no idea what I was getting myself into. Complicated things tend to be that way. Sure, we're always hoping for the best. We always want to see the best in people and situations. Trust me, I didn't intend to drive through almost 5 feet of water today. And I'm sure you didn't plan on being stuck in a complicated situation either.

Reflection Journal:

Chapter 12 From Perplexity to Peace

Hey Friend,

If you've made it this far... first of all... I'm proud of you.

You've walked through the confusion, the heaviness, the questions.

You've faced the mountains, named the joy thieves, sat in the storms.

And now?

Now we talk about peace.

Not the fake kind you can buy for $9.99 on a motivational poster.

Not the kind you have to force with toxic positivity.

I mean the real, deep, bone-level peace that only comes when you've

wrestled through the mess and still found God sitting with you in it.

Peace Isn't the Absence of Chaos

Let's get one thing straight... peace doesn't mean everything in your life suddenly gets tied up with a neat little bow.

Peace isn't having any problems.

Peace is presence... God's presence.

It's the steadiness you feel even when the storm is still rumbling off in the distance.

Peace is being able to say:

"I don't have all the answers... but I know the One who does."

Couch Talk: The Peace You Can't Explain

There have been moments when nothing outside me changed:

- The bills were still unpaid.

- The relationships were still messy.

- The future was still unknown.

And yet... deep in my chest... peace showed up anyway.

Not because the circumstances got easier.

Because God got louder in my spirit.

Philippians 4:7 calls it the:

"peace that surpasses all understanding."

It doesn't always make sense.

It doesn't have to.

From Perplexity to Peace

If perplexity is the messy middle, peace is the quiet confidence that the Author of your story hasn't dropped the pen.

It's the reminder that:

- You're not forgotten.

- You're not forsaken.

- You're not stuck... you're being shaped.

The questions may not have easy answers.

The healing may still be in progress.

The road ahead might still be winding.

But you can walk it in peace.

You can breathe easy, even here.

A Blessing Over You

If you hear nothing else from me, hear this:

You are not a failure because you're confused.

You are not broken because you're tired.

You are not alone because you're hurting.

You are loved.

You are being led.

You are being prepared.

And peace... real peace... is closer than you think.

Final Prayer

Lord,

Thank You for meeting me in the mess.

Thank You for the peace that doesn't depend on circumstances.

Help me to walk forward with confidence,

even when the path feels uncertain.

Teach me to rest in the truth that I am never alone... not in my

confusion, not in my fear, not in my becoming.

I trust You... fully, finally, even here.

Amen.

Anchor Verse

"You will keep in perfect peace those whose minds are steadfast, because they trust in you."

- Isaiah 26:3

Reflection Questions

- What does peace mean to you right now... not what it should mean, but what it really feels like?

- Where in your life do you feel God asking you to trust Him more deeply?

- Write a letter to your future self... 5 years from now. Tell them what you're proud of, what you're fighting through, and what you hope they never forget about this season of your life that you made it through.

Space to Reflect

Use the following blank pages to expand on these questions or anything that is weighing you down. Once you're finished, take 3 deep breaths. I know that this time of reflection will bring you clarity.

A Letter to the Reader Who Stayed

Hey You,

You made it.

Maybe you didn't sprint. Maybe you crawled. Maybe you paused a dozen times along the way.
But you stayed.

You stayed through the messy middle.

You stayed when the questions didn't have easy answers.

You stayed even when it would've been easier to give up.

And that tells me something about you... something important:

You are stronger than you know.

You are more courageous than you feel.

You are more deeply loved than you can even imagine.

Life won't always be clear.

The road ahead will still have its twists and turns.

But here's what I want you to hold onto:

Confusion is not your identity.

Perplexity is not your end.

You are not stuck... you are becoming.

You are not forgotten... you are being formed.

If you leave this book with anything, I hope it's this:

You are still worthy in the in-between.

You are still held in the complicated.

You are still becoming in the mess.

Stay open. Stay soft. Stay willing to believe that peace is still possible... even here, even now, even when it doesn't make sense.

I'm proud of you. I'm cheering for you.

I'm sitting right here with you, on this couch we built out of stories and prayers and grace.

And I believe with all my heart:

The best is not behind you. It's ahead.

With love and hope,

- **Christina**

A Blessing for the Road Ahead

Hey... before you go, let me leave you with this:

I hope you leave these pages knowing you don't have to have it all figured out.

You don't have to rush your healing.

You don't have to fake a smile or tie your story up with a pretty bow.

It's okay to still have questions.

It's okay to be in the middle of becoming.

It's okay not to know where this road is taking you.

But I hope you believe this...

even when it's quiet, even when it's hard, even when it doesn't make sense:

You're not lost.

You're not forgotten.

You're not too late or too far gone.

You're held.

You're seen.

You're loved... right here, in the in-between.

So take a deep breath.

Take the next small step.

Trust that peace isn't waiting for you at the finish line... it's been

walking with you this whole time.

Go gently.

Go honestly.

Go knowing you're not alone.

At the beginning of this book, I encouraged you to seek professional help. I don't say that because I think you can't handle it on your own. Trust me, I'm like the poster child for trying to do everything on my own. Mainly because I think that people couldn't handle me or possibly understand what I've gone through. Turns out most of us think that way about ourselves.

I didn't realize that until I had gotten myself into therapy to work through many of the issues that I've shared with you in this book. You might not be ready for that type of commitment just yet, but I urge you to reach out to someone. You do not have to go through life by yourself. You do not have to do this alone. I know it might seem like you've made a mistake, and maybe people won't understand or they'll judge you. I promise that everyone has gone through their own personal version of hell. Everyone has done something that they're not proud of. Everyone is hurting.

I heard a quote the other night from one of my gamer friends: Every guy is the biggest proponent of holding it in. So, at least half our population is hiding their feelings of failure because they don't want to be seen as weak.

Friend. You aren't alone. Reach out to someone today. You deserve to be heard. And who knows, you might even figure out some new strategies to help you maneuver through life. If anything, I promise that it'll help you feel better. Now I know that this is like super deep, and why are we doing this on the last chapter of the book, but I just wanted to make sure that I took that moment to reach out to you to ask you to take a stand for yourself. I promise future you will look back on this moment and be like, "that's it, that was when I finally broke through. That was the moment that I started living again."

Let me tell you that is one of the most empowering feelings to have.

Acknowledgments

To the ones who stayed...

Thank you for sitting with me in the questions, for holding space when I had no answers, and for reminding me that healing isn't a straight line.

To the friends who loved me through the messy middle...
Your kindness was a map back to myself.

To the quiet moments, the unanswered prayers, the long nights...
Thank you for teaching me that confusion can be a classroom, not a curse.

To the mountains that looked impossible and the storms I thought would break me...
Thank you for showing me that peace isn't found in the absence of hard things, but right in the middle of them.

And most of all...To the One who sat with me in the silence, caught every tear, and stayed steady even when I wasn't...
This is Yours.

www.ingramcontent.com/pod-product-compliance
Lightning Source LLC
Chambersburg PA
CBHW060138130626
46556CB00006B/2392